FROM THE EAST END TO THE WEST COAST

AND HALFWAY BACK ... *by John Leaney*

The story of a boy from the East End of London and his journey to a successful life in the United States.

THE AUTHOR.

From the East End to the West Coast and Halfway Back' is dedicated to Jack Leaney the author's son, who tragically lost his mother to breast cancer before he ever had a chance to know her. He was reared by his father and, like so many of his fathers' friends, knows nothing of his fathers' former life. One which began as the son of factory workers who lived in a working-class town ten miles from London England, where, like so many others from London's East End, the family relocated after their neighborhood was severely affected by the blitz of World War Two.

Winning a scholarship to one of the best schools in the area completely changed the author's life. Though victimized by a teacher because of his class, the school changed him as he saw the possibilities of a much better life. Defying his parents, and the East End tradition of going straight from school to a job, he attended college where he studied to be a teacher.

After college he taught in Northern England, in one of the worst neighborhoods in the country. He rose quickly to become part of the senior management team and was encouraged to pursue the highest offices in secondary education.

The author was then invited to spend a summer working as a soccer coach in the United States. He grabbed the opportunity and moved there. He established himself as a successful coach at the youth and collegiate levels, working on the west coast for the Mission Bay Soccer Club and at the University of California at San Diego, and later for the Northwest Soccer Club in Minneapolis and at Macalester College in St Paul, Minnesota.

He met his wife Carrie in Minnesota and Jack was born in 2004. She died in 2006. The book is dedicated to Jack in her memory.

TABLE OF CONTENTS

INTRODUCTION... i

ACKNOWLEDGEMENTS.. iii

PART ONE, GROWING UP IN ENGLAND.

MY EARLY LIFE.. 3

DAGENHAM... 5

MY FATHER.. 7

BILL AND GEORGE.. 9

GREYHOUNDS HORSES AND GAMBLING. 11

HORSES DOGS AND HOLIDAYS.. 13

FOOTBALL.. 15

UNCLE ALBERT.. 18

PRIMARY SCHOOL... 21

THE ELEVEN PLUS EXAM.. 24

MY EARLY YEARS AT BARKING ABBEY GRAMMAR SCHOOL. 26

ASPIRATIONS TO STAY ON AT SCHOOL. 30

GOING TO WORK TO STAY ON AT SCHOOL. 32

SIXTH FORM... 38

SCHOOL UNIFORMS. 39

PROBLEMS IN SIXTH FORM... 41

COULD I ATTEND COLLEGE?... 43

LEARNING MY TRADE... 45

PART TWO, COLLEGE AND TEACHING.

FOOTBALL IN COLLEGE...49

COLLEGE OF EDUCATION...51

TEACHING PRACTICE..54

MY FIRST TEACHING ASSIGNMENT...58

A SOCIAL EDUCATION...61

TIME FOR A CHANGE...63

GAINING ACCEPTANCE...65

HOW DIFFERENT COULD TEACHING BE?...67

CRIME AND PUNISHMENT..69

STUDENT TRIPS ABROAD...72

PART THREE, THE UNITED STATES.

NOW FOR SOMETHING COMPLETELY DIFFERENT..77

INTRODUCTION TO COLLEGE COACHING...79

THE MINNESOTA CONNECTION..81

DIVISION III HAS A NEW CHAMPIONSHIP..83

THE FINAL FOUR..86

A FULL TIME COLLEGE SOCCER COACH..88

BOMBSHELL..90

WHERE DO I GO?...91

A TEAM HAPPY TO SEE ME...93

MEANWHILE BACK AT THE RANCH..96

CHANGE..99

STREET SMARTS..101

MEN AND WOMEN IN THE SAME SEASON?..102

SUCCESS MAKES IT MORE DIFFICULT..105

THE GOLDEN YEARS..108

CAN WE WIN A NATIONAL CHAMPIONSHIP?..110

NATIONAL CHAMPIONSHIP...114

SPONSORSHIP..118

REPEAT. 120

REFEREES. 122

NCAA TOURNAMENT SELECTION. 126

THE TIMES THEY ARE A CHANGING. 128

CARRIE. 129

I WILL SEE YOU IN NOVEMBER. 133

WE FIGHT. 137

LIFE GOES ON. 138

A NECESSARY CHANGE. 140

DIRECT OR BLOODY RUDE. 142

JOHN THE PUBLIC ADDRESS MAN. 144

RETIREMENT. 146

INTRODUCTION.

This book is dedicated to you Jack. I hope it will fill in the many missing gaps in your knowledge of our family and my early life.

At the time of writing I am seventy years old and you are fourteen. I have spent approximately half of my life in two countries. I was born and reared in England and moved to the United States at the age of thirty-three. You were born in the United States, so I have adapted a more American style of writing. You will see and be reminded of the phrase, 'England and the United States are two countries separated by a common language.'

If others read this story it is necessary for me to say these are my memories. As we grow older, we all remember things differently. With my memory fading I do not have the time to check every fact with every person, who of course might remember something differently. At no time do I try to distort facts for my benefit. What you read is what I remember,

I hope you enjoy the story,

Dad.

ACKNOWLEDGEMENTS.

Many thanks to the best man at my wedding and author of many books John W Hershey, for his editing skills and advice.

PART ONE,
GROWING UP IN ENGLAND.

MY EARLY LIFE.

I was born on November 18th' 1948 in St. Andrews hospital in Bow, London. One mile from the St.-Mary-le- Bow church. I consider myself a true born cockney. A true born cockney, originally a pejorative term, is somebody born under the sound of Bow bells, the bells of Bow church. When I asked my parents if the bells could be heard at the hospital their answer was "probably, on a clear day." Well considering it is a walk of less than a mile from one to the other, I would think there were many days when the bells could be heard at the hospital.

For the rest of England all people from London are called 'cockneys.' What they fail to realize, unless they ever lived in London, is how different the cockneys are from the rest of the population of London, notably the west, southwest and northwest parts. Bow is in East London, which was the working-class area of the city, with an identity all its own. Recently it has been transformed into something much better. My father was born and reared in Bow, along with six brothers and a sister. My mother was born and reared in the neighboring borough of Whitechapel, along with six sisters and three brothers. Whitechapel was famous as the stomping ground of Jack the Ripper. I know my mother talked about their fears of Jack the Ripper.

She failed to realize he would have been seventy years old when she was a teenager. Still it was understandable, as the 'Ripper' had never been apprehended.

I have no memory of any interaction with my grandfather on my father's side. My mother always said "You must remember him" but I did not. I had a big relationship with my grandmother, however. She moved into our house at Rothwell Road with my uncle Bill, I imagine they had been evicted from their place

The Leaney boys, with father and mother front and center. From the back left to right, Bill, Albert, Ted, Fred. Front row Dave, then father and mother Fred JW Leaney and Mary Leaney, then my father George. Missing is Len killed in World War II, and Beatrice the only daughter.

There was a difficult atmosphere as my grandmother deemed herself the lady of the house, telling us what to do while my mother was at work. There was friction between my mother and my grandmother.

My uncle Bill also lived with us. He had always lived at home with his mother, but now he must have been in his forties. He was later to suffer an industrial accident at work when he was sucked into a large pipe. The force of the accident really messed up his stomach. He was to receive a large sum of money in compensation, but this happened after they left our house. Later he paid for a trip to Australia for my mother and father, so the three of them could visit my uncle Albert.

I would visit my grandmother once a week, once they had found a place to live, not far away in a place called Ilford. I remember she would set three cups and saucers out for tea when there were only two of us. My father told me she was setting the place for my grandfather who had passed away.

They had been separated for a while. My grandfather was living in Ramsgate, on the southeast coast, when news came that he was found dead by his landlady. I can remember my father being disgusted when it was said he had no money on him. He laughed and uttered, "He was always carrying," which was probably true knowing the life he had led. My father was inferring his landlady, who found him, had relieved my grandfather of his cash.

I knew my grandmother and grandfather on my mother's side well. They lived about two hundred miles away in Swindon, a town in the southwestern part of England. The family had been evacuated there in the war and had decided to stay. My brother and I would regularly spend a large part of our summer holidays there. My brother once spent a whole summer in Swindon and came back with a west country accent for a while.

There is an interesting story about my grandfather who served in World War I, where he lost a brother in the carnage. He loved children and would often play with us.

We noticed he had two stumps for fingers on his right hand, where his index and middle finger should have been. He said they were hit by bullets in the war. This was probably true, but it was also true during trench warfare, when infantry was ordered to go over the top of the trenches, some were too afraid and were executed by firing squad for cowardice. It was rumored some would inflict wounds upon themselves to be sent home as casualties. Of course, it would have been impossible to fire a rifle with his injury, so he was sent home. It is hard to know if my grandfather followed the latter course of action, but when my mother was drunk, she would talk about him being a wife beater.

She claimed he would come back from the pub drunk, become angry, and just attempt to assault my grandmother. My mother said all the girls would surround their mother to prevent a wife beating from happening. They would coerce him to sit down in a chair, where he would eventually fall asleep. Many years later my sister was in Swindon one summer holiday and recounts a story of a time when the family noticed he was late coming home. They were nervous and immediately thought he had stopped for a drink, so they started clearing the shelves of potential objects. It turned out he was late because his bike had a puncture.

DAGENHAM.

My time in Bow was short lived. Before I was a year old, the family moved ten miles east along the river Thames, to Dagenham.

Dagenham was where the work was. My father took a job as a lorry driver for Briggs Motors, which was eventually taken over by the Ford Motor Company, making it the largest Ford plant in Europe. I do not know for sure, but I can imagine the job was the reason for the move. Later, I came to believe my mother had something inside her about wanting a better life, so it could have played a part.

She married the son of a bookmaker who at one time owned a club, and who was also not shy of mixing with the wrong company. I am also suspicious she worried about the potential for criminal behavior, something not frowned upon in Bow. I think she wanted a new start.

My earliest memories were of 76 Rothwell Road, Dagenham. I was told later I cried a lot. There were times when my mother was drunk, and she would let out the family secret. I was unwanted, a surprise they could do without. The story goes my father was seriously ill in hospital, when my mother discovered she was pregnant with me.

My dad used to tell a story of waking in the middle of the night and seeing his wife by the bedside crying. He assumed the doctors had asked her to be there because they did not think he would make it through the night. It is said he uttered a phrase, "What are you doing here?" With no answer but sobs he is supposed to have said "Do not worry, I am too wicked to die." He later recovered.

During his illness a common east end scenario might have played out. How can you have an abortion? Abortions were not legal in those days. It was not only expensive to try to do it illegally, but it was also very dangerous.

If my father had a 'win' at the dog track on a Saturday night when my mother was out with him, she would take the opportunity to have the extra drink or two. She could do one of two things when she had too much to drink. She could become sullen and morose and complain about her life, or she could talk about things she never talked about when she was sober. We as children should have been happy after a win because we would all be better off, but we were nervous it sometimes led to arguments.

Here I am at 76 Rothwell Road. It was a house with a huge garden. My parents told me this was a typical picture of me, always crying.

When happily drunk, she would occasionally laugh about how lucky I was to be alive. She would recount the old wives' tales of drinking hot gin and running up and down stairs, actions designed to bring about a miscarriage. She was from the east end of London, famous in the old days as a haunt for some men from the royal family, who it is rumored would frequent ladies of the night in an area nobody really cared about. It must have worked in the past, but obviously it did not work on me. I used this later to describe why I could sometimes be very stubborn.

I was the middle child of three and I felt at times I had 'Middle Child Syndrome.' NBC's Today program once did a story on this 'syndrome'.

Adding second and third children greatly impacts the family structure, and a middle child is created. Yes, the "Middle Child Syndrome" is very real. Middle kids bemoan their fate as being ignored and often grow resentful of all the parental attention given to the oldest and the baby of the family and feel short-shifted. Three children triangulate sibling relationships, with one child at any given point feeling like the odd man out from the chumminess of the other two.

My father was very concerned about the possibility of my brother getting into trouble, and he was at times hard on him. This produced problems with my mother who felt she needed to defend him. Since my father seemed to pay a lot of attention to my sister, the only girl and youngest child, I felt left out. I took out my frustration on my sister and tormented her.

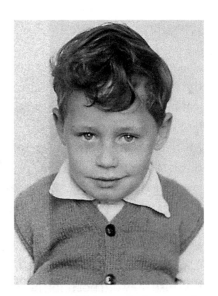

How could you not love such a cute boy?

We were often home alone due to the hours my parents worked. They were factory workers working 8:00 am to 5:00 pm. If we were home together, I would often make fun of her.

I do not think it was out of malice but more out of boredom. It did not last long. By the time I was fifteen or sixteen I was staring at the possibility of leaving school to go to work. If we wanted, we could quite easily not go to school, and our parents would not know.

My earliest memory of school was the day we were to move up from the infant school, or kindergarten, to the primary school. We were told to come to the infant school first, and the teacher would take us across to the primary school. I was shocked as we arrived to see several of the boys had 'disobeyed.' I could see them already playing in the primary school playground. I could not believe they did not obey the teacher's instructions. I always did, but that was to change.

MY FATHER.

My father was typical of the east end of London. If you thought you could get away with something illegal, then why not? He had discovered where the company he worked for discarded their unneeded wood, so a great deal of it somehow found its way into his hands.

My early memories of 76 Rothwell Road include our back yard. Protected by a gate it had rows of sheds. Inside the sheds, which my father built, was a large amount of wood in the form of planks. I assume he built the sheds to store the wood. He was later to build my sister a doll house. This was not the normal small doll house to play with. It was the size of a shed and we could all walk in and play in there. I remember being in a shed where the planks of wood were stored when I asked him about the small indentations on the end of the planks. "Rats," he said. I do not think I went in the sheds again.

We had a smaller wooden enclosure at the end of the garden called the chicken run, where we kept chickens. I assume he built it. For our Sunday dinner, an east end tradition, I remember we ate chicken. My mother cooked it with roast potatoes and vegetables. I assume there were times when the chicken came from our own stock. My brother once asked if I wanted to go out back and watch dad strangle a chicken. I declined.

I remember a time when my dad's eldest brother Ted was visiting. The subject of rats came up and he told me a story of my father from the old days. Apparently, my dad was a good footballer. The story goes he and his brothers had surrounded a rat in the high street in Bow. When the rat made a break for freedom my father is said to have taken a swing at it with his trusty left foot and launched it through a shop window. I remember vividly when uncle Ted left, my father made a point of coming straight to me and saying in a serious manner "Do not believe anything he tells you." Ted apparently was an avid storyteller...or was he?

I can remember dad had made a large wheelbarrow. We had so much wood he decided he could make money selling firewood in the neighborhood. He made bundles of kindling, ideal for starting a fire. None of the houses in our neighborhood were heated in any other way than an open fireplace. My sister and I would take the wheelbarrow full of kindling and we would knock on the doors of our neighbors, who would buy them at two pence a bundle. When we returned, after selling every bundle, my father would collect the money and give us sixpence each.

I also remember a time when he must have had a big win gambling. He bought eight beautiful 'Book of Knowledge' books and presented them to the three of us. They were akin to encyclopedias. We would use them for reference, but he was upset because he rarely saw us reading them. He thought they were books we should read.

He used nicknames for us. Was it possible he did not remember our names? He always called me 'pinhead.' If I did something wrong, he would say "Hey gormless come here." My brother was the big'n, I was the little'n and my sister was 'her' or 'she'.

An incident with my brother is worth telling. He came home one night from his local pub with his face badly beaten. He had been in an argument with a man he would hang with, and they had taken the argument outside. My mother was upset. My father took no notice.

The next night I came home to find my mother alone sobbing helplessly. I asked her what was wrong. She said Michael has gone back to the pub and she was worried he will be in a fight again. I asked where my father was and she said she did not know, she said he had left a short time ago.

It turned out my father was worried my brother would get beaten again by the same man, as a warning to not come back to the pub. My mother said my brother told her he had to go back to the pub to prove he could take a beating, and it was all over and done with. My father, who showed little interest in what had happened, did something we thought was out of character. It turned out to be what one did where he grew up. He had gone to the pub just before closing time to wait outside, out of view. He held an iron bar wrapped in a cloth. If the same person was going to beat up my brother, then my father would deal with him. Nothing happened, but my father never mentioned the story, and my mother made sure I was sworn to secrecy.

Such was life in the east end of London.

BILL AND GEORGE.

Bill and George were the same person, my father. He was christened George, but I never once heard my mother call him by that name. She called him Bill, as did all members of her side of the family.

How he came by the name dates to the Second World War. Up until the time he was drafted my father made his living by gambling and hustling around pool tables. He was a very good pool player. Hustling at pool often meant losing to your opponent early, when the bets were small, and then asking to raise the stakes to try to win the money back. In east end culture it was the person who lost to the hustler who was the fool.

As a newly enlisted soldier he used the same ruse on his immediate superior, his staff sergeant. This man was not an east ender and took exception. He exacted his revenge by doing his best to make my father's army life miserable. At the end of his first leave he faced two choices. He could take the matter into his own hands using physical violence in dealing with the sergeant, or simply not return to base as ordered. Both options meant serving time in the 'glasshouse' as it was called.

He chose the second option. He went 'absent without leave' or AWOL. Since his brother Bill did not qualify for enlistment due to physical ailments, my father adopted his name and used it when he visited my mother and family in Swindon. They all called him Bill and the name stuck.

During the war young couples married because it was possible the young men might not survive the conflict. Plus, by marrying, the wives became eligible for widow's pensions. My parents were no exception. The name Bill Leaney appeared on their wedding certificate. Much later, after my father passed away, my mother grew anxious about the potential legality of their union. She pursued the matter vigorously and discovered the marriage was indeed certified under the law.

I remember a time, much later, telling my father how I planned to hitch hike north to see my college friends in Newcastle. He said I would probably go through Northallerton. He recounted how he spent time in the army prison there, after he finally gave himself up and faced the consequences of his absence.

He told me a funny story about trying to turn himself in. He was broke and standing at a railway station when he saw a soldier on guard duty. He approached the man and said he wanted to report that he was absent without leave. The soldier pleaded with him to go away. My father was surprised but understood when the soldier added "I am off duty in ten minutes, now get lost."

9

When I was young, and on a school holiday, my father often took me with him in his lorry to pick blackberries from bushes at the side of the road. We brought them home and my mother made jam. We grew tired of blackberry jam every day, so my mother kept a secret jar of strawberry jam hidden away, for times when he was not home.

My father often arranged my rides when I needed to return to college in Manchester. The Ford factory had a subsidiary plant in Liverpool and drivers regularly left Dagenham at four in the morning to make the run. The route went right past our home which was on a main road. The ride was free, but the timing was not ideal, plus I was dropped off in North Cheshire and had to hitch hike the short journey to Manchester. However inconvenient, it saved money and I needed every penny as I worked my way through college. My dad instructed me that if the driver stopped for tea, I needed to offer to pay.

Always the speculator, my father was very creative when it came to the possibility of extra money. When he made the long trip to Liverpool, he was given a travel allowance to cover meals and an overnight stay in a guest house. Sometimes he pocketed the money and drove from Liverpool to Swindon to stay at my grandmother's house, where of course he was fed. He returned to Dagenham the next day but his route had taken him about 150 miles out of his way just so he could save the hotel and meal money.

GREYHOUNDS HORSES AND GAMBLING.

We would laugh at home and say our father loved animals. He certainly spent a great deal of money on greyhounds and horses. For as long as I can remember, I cannot think of any other hobby he enjoyed, except betting on dogs and ponies.

I cannot say however he suffered from a gambling addiction, because it would mean he belonged to the group of people who lost everything and more, due to their problem. When my father lost all the money he possessed at the time, he might borrow small amounts from my mother or me, but he in no way hurt us financially. We could have been better off of course but he would always work overtime, and he paid us back immediately after he received his paycheck. The debate sometimes would be between my mother and father as to how much he owed her.

It stemmed from what usually happened on a Saturday evening. My father loved to go to Romford Greyhound Stadium, and my mother would enjoy going because she could have a drink in the bar. Also, win or lose, she insisted on going for a drink afterwards.

My father was not a big drinker. He would try to go to the greyhound track without my mother, but to no avail. If he left it late and suggested he would go for the last few races, it would not work. My mother could be dressed in a minute. There was no way for him to go without her. He would sometimes sit there until it was quite late, and my mother would ask him if he wanted to go. He would then say he had no money. She would give him some money, and this was to cause arguments later. My mother expected to be paid back, but my father thought it was a gift because she was the one who wanted to go.

A problem occurred if he won, which he rarely did, because my mother would drink more. I think he resented it and arguments began.

When I came home from playing football on a Saturday morning, I witnessed a familiar sight. Our small front room had newspapers open all over the floor. Dad was hard at work studying the form of the horses in the televised races. Generally, these races were handicapped. This is where all the horses carried differing weight cloths designed to give every horse in the race an equal chance.

These were the hardest races to predict. My father also bet in doubles, trebles and accumulators.

It was very difficult to win, but if he did, it would be a lot of money from a small stake. It seems he was more interested in watching his bets on television than using a more scientific approach, picking short odds favorites in races that were not televised.

In one of our rare conversations he told me if he was a full-time gambler, he could make money. London at that time had many greyhound tracks. He said a professional gambler would study all the races at all the tracks in London running on a certain day. He would pick what he thought were two stone wall certainties and would set off to put a large amount of money on one dog at one track. He would then do the same at the next track and come home. I really think he believed that was either too much work, or not enough fun.

I had to laugh one day. In order that my mother would not know how much he won, he sometimes hid money after a win. I remember a day when he was moping around the house, so he went out to the shed and suddenly came running back in. It was obvious he had found a hidden pile of money. He was off to the betting shop in minutes.

HORSES DOGS AND HOLIDAYS.

The Ford Motor Company determined the timing of employee vacations and my father was given two weeks paid leave in July, when the company shut down operations for a fortnight.

The fifties and sixties were also a time of labor unrest. Strikes were numerous and there were even rumors of communist infiltration of the unions. Once, after the union won a significant pay raise, my father's vacation time was also increased to three weeks. My father did not appreciate the strikes. Though he received some pay from the union funds it was barely enough to survive. He told me how pointless it was to go out on strike and shared the mathematics with me. Once the strike was settled, he claimed it took him two years to replace the money lost by not working, at which time the workers would strike again. He did not go to the meetings where a vote was taken. It was rumored if you voted against the strike you could be approached by a shady character suggesting you put your hand down.

Times were hard but we survived. There was always enough food on the table but of course we were denied anything else we might want or need. During the designated factory shut down we went on holiday. We frequented two places: Shoeburyness and Brighton.

Shoeburyness was a mile or two from Southend, the most popular of resorts for the factory workers. Although we considered Shoeburyness to be the seaside, it was really the 'Thames estuary,' where the river flowed into the North Sea. Sometimes, when we went swimming, we ran into problems. I remember being so proud of my new white swimming trunks until I came out of the water one time and noticed oil on them. The other resort Brighton was on the south coast, sixty miles south of London.

As children we did not understand why we went to Shoeburyness and Southend. They were the destinations that working families could afford. We were just glad it was the seaside. When the tide was out many people walked into the estuary to pick up shellfish. Cockles and muscles were abundant and considered 'working class fare.' A famous stand in the market area of the east end of London was 'Tubby Isaacs,' who sold nothing other than shellfish gleaned from the area we swam in.

There was an incident one time that I will never forget. A storm was brewing, and my brother Michael had gone out looking for shellfish. We could not see him or shout to him to come in. My father went out into the estuary to fetch him. By the time he found him and brought him back to the car the storm was raging. There was no time to drive anywhere, so my father drove the car up to a small tree and parked it there to shelter from the strong winds. There was a distinct possibility without any shelter the car could have been blown away.

We only went to Shoeburyness on days when the nearby Southend greyhound stadium provided evening racing. Children were also allowed in. Afterwards my mother's needs were met when we adjourned to a pub called 'The Hole in the Wall' which had a garden where children could join their parents.

I remember one time when my mother's friend Ellen Bedford, her husband Joe and their son Johnny, my best friend, were with us. We were driving back from Southend, about an hour's drive, when they stopped at a pub about halfway home. Johnny and I were left in the car outside to amuse ourselves. We were playing a game of hide and seek. While Johnny went to hide, I went through a pretend routine of starting the car, taking the hand brake off, driving left and right before putting the hand brake back on. This would give Johnny enough time to hide. One time I got out of the car without setting the hand brake. The pub was at the top of a big hill and the car started rolling forward. I immediately jumped back in and secured the hand brake, but the car had visibly moved about five yards. Johnny and I spent an hour waiting for our parents, convinced somebody would notice the car was out of position in the parking lot. They came out of the pub laughing and joking and did not notice. We breathed a huge sigh of relief.

The other resort, Brighton, was on the south coast about sixty miles south of London. Brighton was truly on the sea, albeit the English Channel. The strange thing for us as kids was the fact that we thought beaches were sandy. Brighton's beach is filled with stones. These stones are beautifully smooth and round due to millions of years of waves washing them back and forth. The sea was salty, however. But we knew we were there for the races.

The Brighton race meeting lasted three days. I think our stay depended on my Dad's good fortune. My mother was smart enough to keep money away from him until he needed it. I do remember one time leaving the bed and breakfast house when he started rushing us. I am not sure, but I think he had the money ready to pay but could not see the landlady. The thought of more money to gamble that day may have predicated a 'runner.'

One of the saddest stories I heard after we moved from Rothwell Road was about my friend Johnny Bedford's sister Josie. She was young when she married a man who was a crane driver. We heard he was killed in a crane accident not very long after the wedding.

It was not long afterwards we heard another sad story. Josie was walking down the street with her father Joe when he suddenly had a heart attack and died in front of her. She was such a sweet girl and we all felt for her.

FOOTBALL.

I was good at football, but it was my uncle Albert who came to see me play on Saturday mornings for my school team. On Saturday mornings my father studied the day's racing form. I remember playing up a year as the only nine-year old on a very good team for the size of the school I attended, Monteagle.

The local newspaper, the Barking Advertiser, sponsored a knockout tournament for all the primary schools in Barking. I remember our huge semifinal game with Manor, the local powerhouse. We played to a 3-3 tie in the first game but beat them 3-0 in the replay.

This set up the final, the first game at a new small stadium in the area. For a small school like Monteagle it was massively important to us. Even my father put down his racing form and came to the game which we won 1-0.

I can remember the walk home with dad and uncle Albert. Suddenly, they started arguing. I can remember to this day what they said. Uncle Albert said out loud "How dare you criticize him when you have never seen him play."

Our area played a good brand of football. One of the teams we knocked out in the early rounds was Ripple Road. A player who played for them at the time was Trevor Brooking, now Sir Trevor, an English legend. I played against him many more times in high school when I played for Barking Abbey, and he played for Ilford County High. We would greet each other before the high school games. He, of course went on to great things, but I still remember he played for his high school, even while he was an apprentice professional at West Ham United.

His improvement was meteoric. They beat us in one game 4-1. He scored all four.

After the final, I am posing. My father is top left looking for me.

A funny story from this relationship is worth sharing. I think we were about fifteen years old. We did not have coaches in those days.

Our captain gave the pre match speech in the prefect's room where we changed before games. We had no locker rooms or showers. During the speech he told us the opposing team had a schoolboy international playing for them.

The usual ritual for Trevor and me was to meet at midfield before the game and say hi. When there, he saw me looking past him at the rest of his team and said, "John, who are you looking for?" I replied that I heard there was a player on his team who had been selected for England schoolboys. He laughed and said "John, that player is me."

I was very embarrassed, but we did not get local newspapers at home, so I did not know. He went on to a great career while I became just another good amateur level player.

School football at Barking Abbey was not like other schools. I played for Monteagle for two years at age ten and eleven. When I passed the eleven plus exam, which determined my placement in secondary school at Barking Abbey, we did not play competitive football the first two years.

I am not sure it was the same at other schools, but in my third year at the school we had an under fourteen team which played other schools in the surrounding area.

I soon discovered the under fourteen team I played on, was in fact under fifteen. I was the only player of the correct age. I can only deduce we were such a small elitist type school it had been impossible to compete against the other schools in the area. Nobody seemed to talk about it. We did not dominate, far from it, but at least we were competitive. Our gym teacher Ron Gould was probably tired of the negative results. Ron was later to have an impact on my future.

Around this time, I joined a group called the 'Life Boys.' This was a junior version of the 'Boys Brigade.' I think a friend asked me to go, and at first, I was only interested in playing football for them. It sometimes meant playing two games on a Saturday, but I did not mind.

The team was organized by a man known to me as Reg. There was a part of being a member of the Life Boys that meant we were supposed to attend church on Sundays. Reg encouraged me to go to Sunday school.

He took a great interest in me. He would ask if I wanted to go on a day trip to London to see the sights. One would think my parents might be concerned and ask what was going on, but if they were concerned, they did not say or do anything. Reg might have been 'grooming' me, but nothing untoward happened. I think he was a lonely single man, but it was strange he only took 'me' to see the sights and no other boy in the group.

With going to the Life Boys every Friday night came the responsibility of going to church, or Sunday school as it was for the younger children. It certainly had some effect on me, and eventually it affected my parents. They did not discourage me, because they did not take nearly enough interest in what their children were doing. I did notice however, that they toned down the foul language commonly used in our house.

I am sure they heard me singing my prayers on my knees, before I would have to jump into bed, and the freezing cold sheets. Once in bed I pretended I was an athlete running in a desperate attempt to get warm. Since we had no heat, I could see my breath rising in my bedroom.

My sister slept in the same room as my parents. As we grew older this became a problem.

UNCLE ALBERT.

It would be remiss of me not to talk about the profound effect my uncle Albert had on me. When we were living at Rothwell Road, he would often drop in. He usually brought something for my mother and he always pressed money, (usually a half a crown in the old currency) into my hand when he left.

He was a single man who absolutely loved children. Later in life he married and reared four children of his own. Although he lavished attention on my siblings and me, it was clear I was his favorite because I played football. He came to watch me play and always encouraged me. He often took me to watch Arsenal or West Ham play. I remember asking my dad what professional team was the nearest to us in Dagenham. He said, "West Ham," and that was it. I have been a lifelong 'Hammers' supporter ever since.

Albert often took me to places. Here we are feeding the pigeons at Trafalgar Square in London.

Albert would also take us to London, about ten miles away, where we would see all the sights. He treated us to dinner in a restaurant, something our parents never did. I felt very sad when he decided to move to Australia at a time when Australia encouraged immigrants, by offering what was known as 'assisted passage'.

For ten pounds, probably the equivalent of twenty dollars today, he sailed on a ship with many other passengers, who were also looking to start a new life. The ship took several weeks to reach Australia. His new life began on the ship, when he met his future wife Edie. Two of their four children were to become Olympic athletes.

Albert had two sons and two daughters. His daughters showed athletic potential and he coached them from an early age. When it was clear they were competing at a high level, and had Olympic potential, he arranged for them to have professional instruction.

Anne, the older of the two, was a very accomplished middle-distance runner, winning at the highest level in Australia. The younger sister Margaret followed in Anne's footsteps and eventually made the 1996 Olympic team when the games were staged in Atlanta, in the United States, the country where I lived.

I immediately set about planning arrangements to go to Atlanta. One of my former college players, Matt Jackson, was living there, so I arranged to stay with him.

Albert and I agreed to meet in the stadium, where we watched Margaret qualify for the final in the 1500 meters. Albert and I spent some time together and then watched his daughter take fifth place in the final.

He and I were disappointed that in the results below it lists his daughter as Margaret Crowley, as she had only recently married. It was the first time Albert saw her name on a results board without the name Leaney. Later that evening we watched Margaret ride in a horse drawn carriage in a parade down the main street in Atlanta. Afterwards I called my mother from a local pay phone. After a couple of minutes, I handed the phone to uncle Albert. He came back in tears. All he could say was "Your mother and I had such a special relationship." Later in 2000, when her sister Anne came out of retirement and qualified to run in the 5000 meters at the Sydney Olympics, it was the first time any sisters represented Australia at track and field athletics.

A story from Anne indicates how one cannot change some youthful ways. Albert was in a situation where he did not have enough money to make a house payment, and the family faced eviction. His solution was to put what money he had left on a racehorse at a local track. The horse duly won, and his family was saved.

It was wonderful to connect with Albert again after all the years. We had something in common, we both left our native countries to pursue our dreams, and we both succeeded in our pursuits. I heard just before he died, he asked after me and my newborn son.

Here I am with Albert at the Olympics in Atlanta where we watched Margaret run.

RANK	NAME ATHLETE	FINAL	SEMI	HEAT
1.	Svetlana Masterkova (RUS)	**4:00.83**	4:10.35	4:09.88
2.	Gabriela Szabo (ROU)	**4:01.54**	4:09.83	4:07.32
3.	Theresia Kiesl (AUT)	**4:03.02**	4:09.44	4:09.24
4.	Leah Pells (CAN)	**4:03.56**	4:06.26	4:13.17
5.	Margaret Crowley (AUS)	**4:03.79**	4:06.21	4:07.51
6.	Carla Sacramento (POR)	**4:03.91**	4:06.70	4:13.57
7.	Lyudmila Borisova (RUS)	**4:03.56**	4:06.89	4:13.29
8.	Małgorzata Rydz (POL)	**4:05.92**	4:10.77	4:07.51
9.	Gwen Griffiths (RSA)	**4:06.33**	4:11.12	4:10.80
10.	Regina Jacobs (USA)	**4:07.21**	4:06.13	4:07.41
11.	Kelly Holmes (GBR)	**4:07.46**	4:05.88	4:07.36
12.	Anna Brzezińska (POL)	**4:08.27**	4:07.17	4:11.06

PRIMARY SCHOOL.

I spent four years at Monteagle primary school and two things were unusual about the experience. First, the boys and girls were separated. I was in a class of thirty boys. The girl's classroom was on the other side of the building. Second, I had the same teacher for all four years, Ron Newberry.

For three years I was an excellent student, and at the end of term exams I finished first, top of the class. In my fourth and final year I think I slipped to fourth. A new member of the class finished first, and I was disappointed not to at least have finished second. I cannot think of any reason for not doing so well, but my educational performance was about to change in secondary school, for reasons that will be explained later.

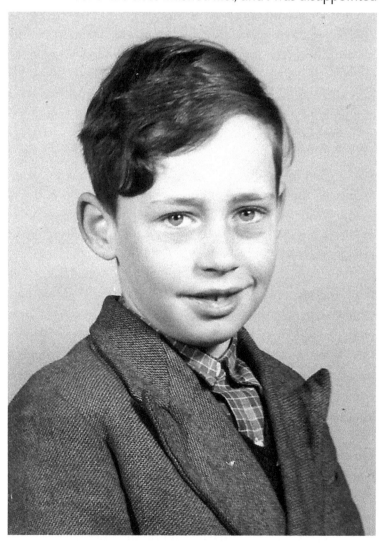

Ron had our classroom seating arranged in four vertical columns. These columns were ability streams. I was in the first column and I sat in the first desk.

Ron seemed like a good teacher, but he had a violent temper. The weaker boys academically were on the other side of the classroom. They included some who in modern times would have probably been placed in special education classes. They needed far more attention than we did. It seemed Ron did not have enough patience with these boys. He preferred to spend his time with the brighter members of the class.

Ron was not shy of using his hand to apply a quick smack across the head to any disobedient boy. There was one incident I have never forgotten. A boy named Barry Sanders was talking out of turn, and Ron

A school photo in my hand me down coat.

was in one of his moods. He quickly strode down the aisle and administered a sharp slap across the head. Barry erupted with the words "You bloody bully." Ron grabbed him and tried to pull him out of his seat. The desks however were not separated from the chairs, they were combined. In pulling Barry out he turned the whole desk over. He then dragged the boy to the door and threw him out. We could still hear Barry outside the door screaming abuse, until Ron opened it and Barry ran off. You could hear a pin drop in our classroom.

It was in primary school I was introduced to boxing. I cannot remember why I participated because I was much smaller than the other boys.

I remember being matched up according to our weight, but I still ended up boxing with boys bigger and heavier than me. Our instructor Percy Rushden only seemed to yell one command to us when we boxed. "Left, left, left" he would shout. That was a problem, I was a southpaw.

Not wanting to disappoint him I would throw my left out from my southpaw stance, thus opening me up to the straight jab of my opponents. I did not last long at this sport. One of my friends Patsy Jacobs did not last long either. We thought he was a tough kid, but he was being 'schooled' by a boy with very good technique. This boy put a straight left into Patsy's face over and over. Suddenly Patsy just lost it. He screamed and waved his arms like a windmill, running at his opponent. The fight had to be stopped.

Ron also introduced us to chess, the game he loved. At the end of every day we all played chess for about half an hour. The better players were moved to the front, where Ron moved from desk to desk playing each of us in turn. I was usually at the front.

Ron invited me to go to his chess club. I was only ten years old, but my parents had no problem with me taking the tube train to Upminster, about ten miles away, where Ron lived. He met me at the station and escorted me to his club, where I played chess against some of his friends. It became apparent he considered me to be a good player. He wanted to show off one of his star pupils. I also remember he invited me to his house for dinner one night, after which we played chess.

Ron asked five or six of the better players in our class to go to the 'London Junior Chess Championships,' which were held during one of our breaks from school and lasted a whole week, Monday to Friday. There were well over a hundred boys participating, and we were arranged in rows. Match winners moved up one row, losers moved down. I moved up quickly. My friends were not so successful, and they were getting bored. After we finished chess each day, we spent time on the underground going to all the places we could, to see the sights of London. We had been issued passes for the underground and bus system, as it was cheaper for the week than paying each fare. It meant we could go anywhere.

I moved up the chess ladder daily until I reached the top groups, where using a chess clock was required. Games at this level took much longer, as the better players tended to deliberate more.

My friends all finished their games before me and came to watch my game. They kept nudging me and made it known we should be having fun on the underground. It became clear to me I was now playing against skilled opponents and it would only be a matter of time before I lost. At least that is what I told myself, as I resigned once I thought I was not doing so well. I did not want to disappoint my friends eagerly waiting to go have fun. I always regretted that action, I would rather have played to the end and lost.

When I arrived at my secondary school I immediately asked if they had a chess club. It turned out they did, and I caused a stir. I found out where the club met, and I joined in. I was twelve years old and had more chess experience than many of the older boys in the club. I caused a problem by beating an older boy, so the secretary who was eighteen years old, and in the upper sixth form as it was called, came to play me. I beat him and immediately found myself playing the club president, who was also in the upper sixth. When I beat him, they both played me, consulting with each other before they finally beat me.

The school had a chess team and I was immediately selected. There were five older boys and me. I played as number five because I think they were probably embarrassed to put me higher. Barking Abbey had a chess trophy called the Blake Cup. The first time I played I lost in an early round and it was a surprise. In my second year I was far more interested in playing football in the playground with the bigger boys. My interest in chess gradually waned. Who would have predicted after my first year at Barking Abbey, I would leave this school at eighteen years of age, without ever winning the Blake Cup?

THE ELEVEN PLUS EXAM.

A lot has been written about the positives and negatives of the eleven plus exam. It most definitely had a profound effect on the three children in our family, affecting us all in different ways.

The eleven plus exam was designed to place children for their secondary education at three different types of school. The highest achievers went to grammar school, the second highest went to a technical high school, and those who achieved the lowest scores went to a secondary modern school.

From my experience I think I am right in saying that within the grammar school group there was another hierarchy. The three children in our family could not have had more different experiences with their secondary education. In my opinion my sister, brother and I have always been equal in intelligence, but we expressed it in different ways.

My brother can take a car apart and put it back together, whereas I have trouble changing a light bulb. My sister is an expert in training horses and dogs. I have a proven record in teaching and coaching.

However, our experience of the ramifications of the eleven plus exam could not be more opposite.

Michael was assigned to George Green's Grammar School in Poplar, part of the east end of London we had left. It was a long journey for him. Because of this people deduced he must have only just passed the exam, and it was mentioned his age was a factor. Michael was one of the youngest in his year. If he had been born six days later, he would have been in the younger class as an older boy, a privilege my November birthday gave me.

Michael was never happy at school. The age for leaving school back then was fifteen, but if you attended a grammar school you could not leave until sixteen. The exception was if you paid a fee of five pounds. My mother duly agreed to do that for Michael, who immediately went to work in an office in the city of London. His life at the school was one of long bus journeys both there and back. He had no schoolfriends living anywhere near him.

My teachers must have thought highly of my prospects after I passed the eleven plus. When it came to the selection of the three schools I might want to attend in an order of preference, I was encouraged to put Barking Abbey as number one.

It was debatable if Dagenham County High, my second choice was nearer. Our house at Rothwell Road was on the west side of Dagenham, very near to Barking. My third choice was Robert Clack Technical High school.

Robert Clack was where my best friend Johnny Bedford had gone the year before. My teachers would probably have considered it a safety school, in case I performed poorly in the exam.

The eleven plus exam had become the subject of much controversy. Many people felt too much rode on the results, and it was too much pressure for children who were only ten years old. An experiment, started in our year, was to not inform the children they were taking the eleven plus exam, thus reducing the pressure. The teachers were supposed to find a way to have the children take the exam as just another test. What a joke!

I remember the head teacher coming into our classroom and reading out names. He told these boys they were going to do something different today.

The eleven plus was optional, so it was clear to all we were going somewhere to take this exam. If anybody did not suspect this, they should not have taken the exam.

We arrived in the main hall, with desks set so far apart, it was clear to all what was about to take place.

Another issue with taking an exam at ten or eleven years of age was of gender. Everybody knows at ten years old girls are far more mature than boys. This was also true in the sphere of education. My sister Pat passed the exam. However, she was one of many girls denied the opportunity of going to a grammar or technical school, in order to maintain gender balance in the classroom.

She transferred later to Dagenham County High, a grammar school, to complete her education. I was the one who was to benefit the most, but not after many trials and tribulations.

Me with my sister Pat.

MY EARLY YEARS AT BARKING ABBEY GRAMMAR SCHOOL.

"Winning a scholarship" as it was called, to Barking Abbey Grammar School changed my life completely. I remember my Monteagle teachers being ecstatic when they found out I was attending, what was reputed to be, the best school in the area of Barking, Ilford and Dagenham. To start with there were two classes of thirty boys and girls. I noted later there was no other boy from my primary school Monteagle in the entire school, and it surprised me that there were only two other boys from Dagenham in my year. They were both in the other class. Being the only boy in my class from Dagenham meant I was to be noticed...because of my accent.

There are different dialects in England, and some are quite difficult to understand. In London it was all the same accent, but *how* you spoke was differentiated by your social class. We define the classes as upper middle, middle, and working class. Londoners know the difference. For example, all royalty from the Queen down speak with a certain accent, and believe they are a class alone. Then there is the upper class who are *not* royalty who emulate this accent. The accent most portrayed on television is that of the middle class.

The working class not only had an accent deemed as somewhat uneducated they also used many words differently.

The first teacher I encountered at Barking Abbey was my first form teacher, Miss E.M. Sheppard. She was known out of earshot by everybody as 'Emma'. She spoke with the accent portrayed by the upper class. She was not a good teacher. Rumor had it she was one of many female teachers hired to replace the men during the war years. I suppose if they did not want to leave, then out of gratitude some were kept on.

The head teacher at Barking Abbey was Mr. Young, known to us as 'Frank'. He was a war hero. It was rumored he was one of the *'few'* as they were known. The pilots who fought the 'Battle of Britain' in the skies over England and the English Channel.

He molded the school into the best in the area, making it somewhat resemble old public schools. We had 'houses' charged with 'Latin' names. Benedict, Charterhouse, Citeaux and Clugny. We had a prefect system. Teachers wore gowns indicating that they had university degrees. This was meant to demonstrate they were more qualified than teachers who went to teacher training colleges, emerging with a teaching certificate, but not a degree.

Significantly Emma would have loved to have worn a gown, but she was not qualified, and it was doubtful she had any teacher training. She only taught first year classes. Emma quite simply did not teach us. She would tell us to read and copy notes from books. She would then amuse herself asking questions. Questions that had nothing to do with schoolwork.

It was clear from day one my accent stood out as working class. The rest of the class were predominantly children from the middle class. Emma focused in on me. There was one boy, Gregory, who spoke with a similar accent to her. I remember Emma saying while we were copying from books, "Oh Gregory, what does your father do for a living?" "He works in a bank, miss" came the reply. It was immediately followed by "Oh Leaney, and what does your father do for a living?" I would answer "He is a lorry driver miss."

The implications were clear. What she in fact did was to get the other members of the class to feel sorry for me. They were smart enough to know what was going on. She was turning me into a rebel, who was becoming popular, mostly with the girls, because he was being abused.

In my first year my schoolwork often depended on the teacher. In Emma's class I was rarely given a good grade. The rest of the class was always anxious to see what she had written on my work, as they witnessed me being singled out. I would not have been an academic star at this school but, left alone, I would have been fine.

There were exams at the end of the year, and I finished in the lower middle of my class. My position was enhanced by my ability at French. This was a completely new subject for me, and I loved it. The class was asked once who had the best French accent and they voted for me. I finished first in the French exam. When Emma announced this, there were positive murmurs from the class, as everybody looked to see my reaction. I did my best to show a little surprise on my face and she jumped all over me. "Leaney, stop boasting!" she yelled. It clearly perturbed her that because of her treatment of me my classmates were showing support, because they recognized what was going on.

Emma only taught first year classes, so it was a relief to move into the second year. However, during this year my family moved from one side of Dagenham to the other. There were several possibilities for the reason behind the move.

We lived in council housing, which meant we paid rent to the local council. Our house only had two bedrooms. My sister was now ten years old and still sleeping in the same room as her parents. My mother petitioned for a house with three bedrooms and put our name on a waiting list.

We were offered a house with two bedrooms on the other side of Dagenham. My mother took it because a downstairs room could qualify as the third bedroom. As a young boy, who did not understand why my sister needed a bedroom, I was devastated. By moving I was going to lose my best friend Johnny Bedford, but what also mystified me was my mother's best friend was Johnny's mother. Why would she leave to go somewhere further from her work and not know anybody? My brother was also affected. The move meant he now had much farther to go to school, as did I. My sister also changed schools. My mother started taking the bus to work when she previously walked. It made no sense to the children, but I have another potentially plausible reason.

Directly across the street from us in Rothwell Road lived a large family who went by the last name of 'Van Kassel'. It was not their real name. The father was a strange man who apparently fancied himself an artist. He had nine children with the three eldest being teenage girls.

Although not obvious to the children in our family, my parents noticed strange cars arriving and leaving in the evenings. First, the eldest girl became pregnant, then her sister. It was obvious to any neighbors Mr. Van Kassel was renting his daughters for prostitution. The question was, did my mother initiate the move and take a house which really did not have a third bedroom, to leave the area? It turned out the question was valid because we moved again within a year, to a house with three bedrooms just around the corner.

I now lived much further from Barking Abbey and had moved twice. It was not an excuse for my poor academic performance. Now in our third house we still did not have heat, so there was nowhere for me to do my homework. The only warm room was the front room, where everybody huddled round the fire and watched television. For a while I studied in the kitchen, but I was constantly disturbed by an English family's dependence on cups of tea.

I found a way round it. I went to school much earlier. I befriended Harry the school caretaker. He opened a classroom for me to do my homework before the other students began to arrive. This also allowed me to join the early crowd of older boys who played football in the school yard.

One of the charges levelled at me from teachers was the one claiming I needed to play with children my own age. I was friendly and hung out with older boys all the time. This stemmed from football. As soon as the bell rung for recess, the footballers made a mad dash to the school yard. They were all older boys, but I could more than hold my own when it came to playing football in the yard with a tennis ball.

Of course, my ability gave me credibility with the older boys, and I started to hang out with them more than with the boys my own age. I managed to survive with minor problems until my fourth year, when another teacher saw me as a real problem.

There were two classes of thirty in each year and in our year the two could not be more opposite. Our class was lively, full of an inquiring sort of energy. Some teachers loved us because of this energy in the classroom, and a good teacher could handle it. The other class was quiet and obedient and rarely in trouble.

I remember Mrs. Young, a teacher who embraced us by joining in our lively discussions. There were times when she literally could not stop laughing, but she always had the ability to reign us in. Then there was 'Taffy.'

We could tell from day one of our fourth year there had been discussions about our class being extremely energetic and sometimes, with some weaker teachers, a little out of control. When Mr. Davies, a man with a strong welsh accent, and known to us as 'Taffy' walked into our classroom, we understood he had probably volunteered to bring more discipline to our class.

At the beginning of every new school year I had always instilled in myself the need for change. I needed to try harder and correct some of my behavioral faults. When I walked into class on the first day of my fourth year, I instinctively went to the back of the class, where I thought I would be less conspicuous. No sooner had Taffy introduced himself than he marched towards me, grabbed a hold of my arm and pulled me out of my seat.

He said, "You, young man, are going to sit where I can keep an eye on you." With that he marched me to the front, signaled to a boy to get out of the desk and deposited me into it, right under his nose. All this was without me doing anything.

I was appalled. He only needed to wait until I misbehaved, but he wanted to make a point. In an instant he had roused my rebellious spirit. In modern times he would have been disciplined. In my mind he had lost me. I was to become a teacher later in life where I learned to wait until a pupil misbehaved before I acted. Sadly, I really liked the subject he taught, geography, and I took it as an elective, later in sixth form.

My fourth year was one of my worst and I virtually owned a seat in Monday night detention, a seat I earned by accumulating poor conduct marks, or if I was bad enough, I earned a straight detention. Four detentions meant a trip to the headmaster's office where a warning was issued. The fifth detention meant corporal punishment. This happened each of the three terms during my fourth year, when I suffered the ignominy of being caned by the headmaster.

ASPIRATIONS TO STAY ON AT SCHOOL.

I started to see the light during my fifth year at Barking Abbey. I now had friends from Ilford and Barking. We rode our bikes after school, and I hung out with them and visited their nice houses.

We never hung out at my house. First there was no room and second, I knew my father would disapprove because he wanted no part of having company in our house. It was beginning to dawn on me that my friends led a better life than I, and I wanted to know what I had to do to have the same.

Most Barking Abbey boys and girls stayed on to sixth form. This was out of the question for me. My mother expected me to do what my brother did: go to work and bring home some money. I was the only fifth year playing on the first team at football, which led me to hang out with the older boys more and more. I started thinking about continuing my education into the sixth form. In order to do that I had to pass O levels, taken towards the end of the fifth year. Everybody at Barking Abbey took as many as eight or nine O levels. Some of the very bright students took one or two of them a year early.

They administered 'mock' exams in the early part of the last term in fifth year. These served as a trial run. Our teachers marked the papers, whereas the real O levels, that came later, were marked by an outside source. The mocks were designed to show you what to expect. They were also expected to accurately predict how you would do in the real exams.

I decided on six O levels, which was low compared to my classmates. There was no help from home, I was on my own. My mother was perfectly prepared to buy me out early, as she had done with my brother, since it meant I could go to work and bring more money into the house.

I took the six mock exams, and I failed five of them. I was disappointed. Though they were not the real exams, I started to think about leaving school at the end of the year and finding a job. What broke my heart was the fact our football team was very good, and I was enjoying it so much I really wanted to stay two more years, if only to play football.

I studied hard and took the real O levels at the end of the term. We expected to receive the results over the summer holidays.

I worked all summer as a lifeguard and brought home good money, part of which I gave to my mother for my 'keep.'

Near the end of summer, I received the results. I remember coming home late from work and my mother handed me an envelope which she had not opened, but the return address and the timing made it clear what it was. I nervously opened it to find out I passed all six O levels. I was eligible to stay on for the sixth form.

My mother was pleased for me as only a mother should be. She did not know I wanted to stay on at Barking Abbey for two more years. I was going to have to wait to bring that up at the right moment. Unfortunately, the right moment never came.

When I did bring up the subject of staying on in sixth form, she would just tell me it was not possible. I was working two jobs while going to

My mother and me at Brighton Races.

school, so I begged her to let me stay on, and offered to give her close to what my brother contributed by working. There was no point in bringing my father into the conversation, he was not the slightest bit interested.

With my mother it was always a question of catching her at the right time. I told her I would work summer jobs. I reminded her it was me who always took the family laundry to the launderette. I was the one who went to the pub every night and stood outside, until a stranger took my money and brought out the bottle of 'Guinness' for her to drink at night. In the end she gave in.

GOING TO WORK TO STAY ON AT SCHOOL.

My family expected me to do what my brother did, but I defied them by staying at school beyond my sixteenth birthday. I was only allowed to do this if I brought money into the house. I had not been a financial burden for some time. I did what many children did for extra cash, I had a paper route. Mine was different than most.

Football is a big thing in England, and they published a Saturday evening paper for the sole purpose of match reports, from the afternoon matches. I had sold these papers since I was thirteen, first working for my brother then taking over his route. Selling the papers required shouting in the streets, to bring people from their houses to buy the paper.

By age sixteen I had turned it into a small business, and I had an idea how to improve it. I kept a notebook and asked buyers if they would like me to deliver the paper to their house. This meant they did not have to listen for me or go outside. They readily agreed, but soon I had too many customers. Some patrons began complaining about how late they received their papers. I decided to employ a friend, paying him half what I made.

Another spin off from the Saturday afternoon football passion was something referred to as 'the pools.' Everybody talked about 'winning the pools' because it involved winning millions, rather like the 'modern day lottery'. It meant predicting eight draws from the approximately ninety professional football games played on a Saturday afternoon. If there were only seven or eight draws, then there was the possibility of one huge winner. If there were many draws, then there would be many winners sharing the pot.

I took a job, all day Sunday, helping a company check the pools, working twelve-hour shifts if there were a lot of draws. I hoped for lots of draws and thus overtime, which could be as much as four hours from six o clock, when we normally finished, until ten o clock. The money increased each hour. There was even the chance to work Monday evenings, which I sometimes did. One night I remember finishing work at ten in the evening and I was so tired I fell asleep on the train home. I missed my station and a guard woke me up at the last stop on the line. It was so late there were no return trains. It cost me my entire four hours of overtime money to pay for a taxi home.

The money I brought in allowed me to stay at school. I remember one of my friends telling my girlfriend how much money I was earning. I think she was disappointed I only took her to the cinema. She could not understand how I was not only giving up half of it as my 'keep,' but I was also responsible for all my expenses, including my bus fares to school, school dinners, and buying my own clothes.

My mother gave my brother some money to make a bike for me. He did a little business in bikes, finding old ones and parts on scrap heaps, then assembling them. He also bought and sold secondhand bikes, so he found or assembled one for me.

This meant I could save on my bus fare. It also meant I could hang out with my school friends who lived a few miles away. I also needed a bike for my rapidly growing paper route. Initially I carried a bag over my shoulder but as it expanded, I needed the bike and rested the bag on the front handlebars.

My friends had much better bikes than I and we talked of riding out much further. When my bike kept breaking down, I started saving for a much better one. When I saved enough, I told my dad about my plan to spend fifteen pounds on a better bike.

He told me to only offer the shop owner twelve pounds and see if he would come down.

School football team, probably Under 15. I am back row second from the left.

This is typical of his east end upbringing. I told the owner my father would not give me more than twelve pounds for the bike. When he did not accept my offer, I felt totally deflated and started walking to the shop door. I thought I was going to lose the bike. I opened the door to go out and the owner shouted at me, "Alright, you can have the bike for twelve pounds." I gave him twelve pounds and rode the bike home ecstatic that I not only bought the bike, but also that my dad's idea had worked.

To stay on in sixth form I had worked summer jobs, but I was determined to have one last summer with my friends and our bikes. We decided to go on a bicycle tour of southwestern England, staying in youth hostels. We even put together a proposal for one of the 'end of school year' prizes which had something to do with a travel award. We did not win, but the teachers in the school collected some money for us.

**Here we are somewhere in the West Country
relaxing during our bicycle tour.**

A few years later, when I was working and off to college, and I was no longer using the bike, my father had a dumb idea. A strange thing happened. Lightning struck our house and the roof was damaged. My dad came up with the idea that we should tell the insurance man my bike was damaged by slates falling off the roof. My father took some bricks and threw them on the bike to damage it, on the chance we could claim money for a new one. When the insurance man came and looked at the bike he said, "I am sorry, personal possessions are only covered if they are inside the house."

When my mother agreed I could stay on at sixth form I also agreed to work to bring in money. Over the next several years of school and college, before I started my first full time job, I worked every summer break. Initially it paid for my keep, but later I needed the money to help me through college.

I spent three summers as a lifeguard and two summers working on the south coast in holiday camps.

The first summer I was lucky to find an opening at the local swimming pool, where they hired me. Apparently, I did not need any qualifications, other than being a strong swimmer. I had not seen a swimming pool like this. I knew it was an open-air pool, as I had often been swimming in it as a young boy. It was an open-air pool in a country famous for long spells of indifferent summer weather. The pool was also one of the largest

I ever experienced. It was fifty-five yards long and twenty-five yards wide, with a huge deck, primarily used for sitting and sunbathing. It did not take long to realize what a great job I had.

The pool was in Barking and was owned and operated by the local authority. As workers, we received the pay scale and benefits given to local authority workers. They had been on strike the previous year and had earned a large pay increase. We were paid by the hour and it was a big jump for me, a college student used to far meagre wages.

What was ideal about this job was the pool was open to the elements; the weather had a huge effect on attendance. We enjoyed many days doing little work when few people came, but when the weather was nice warm and sunny people flocked to the pool, so we worked overtime. I loved the overtime pay so I volunteered every time. A college student like me, who needed money, hoped for good weather. However, it was England and in the summer these weeks were few and far between. The other factor that made this job great for me was times when the weather was not good.

We had enough staff to cover a crowded pool. However, when there were just a few hardy swimmers, we took turns. One or two lifeguards went out to the pool deck, while the rest of us had time to ourselves in our locker room.

I became friendly with my fellow lifeguards, none of whom attended college. They really thought highly of me as a college student, and they allowed me to stay inside during bad weather, because I had summer assignments to finish for the coming semester.

When we were poolside most of us walked around with bare feet. A short while into my second year at this pool, I developed athlete's foot, not unusual for me. I wore tennis shoes and treated the problem, but it very quickly became much worse. It was a more virulent strain and I shed all the skin from both feet. A doctor told me he had not seen anything like my condition in his time in England, only in the far east. My new pink skin was very tender. My feet swelled so much my regular shoes no longer fit me, and I had to wear large boots. Can you imagine my dilemma? A lifeguard, who at the drop of a hat might have to dive in and rescue somebody, is wearing large cumbersome boots.

There was no sick pay however and I needed the work. My friends helped me out by allowing me to stay inside as much as possible. But on really crowded days they needed me. I resolved if a swimmer cried for help near me, I would raise the alarm, and then jump in signaling for help from my fellow workers. It did show however, how little attention our supervisor paid to us. The good news was I only jumped in once, in the shallow end, to rescue a boy pretending he was in difficulty by lying on the bottom of the pool.

I would have loved to return the following summer, but there was no opening because I was not a full-time employee. Instead there was an opening at the other open-air pool in Dagenham.

This was a much smaller pool with no deck for sunbathing. My feet were still tender, so I wore tennis shoes, and nobody seemed to care. There was only me and one other worker, the manager. The pool was not well attended, and if we had bad weather no one came to swim. The manager and I became quite friendly. He often closed the pool early if there was nobody around, which meant of course we were still paid. One

Saturday he looked at me around two o' clock in the afternoon and said, "Do you fancy going to see the Spurs play?" He was a Tottenham Hotspur fan and I was a West Ham fan, and we talked football all the time. I looked at him and said, "But we are open until six o' clock." "Not now," he said showing me the keys "come on let's go."

I also worked two summers at holiday camps. My brother had spent a couple of summers working at one. This was a typically British 'working class' situation. Take a week of entertainment away from home and stay in 'chalets.' I applied to work as a barman. This was a good job because I not only earned money and received tips, but I did not spend money on evening drinking and entertainment, thus I saved more for college.

The camp entertainment was supervised by a Scotsman, his younger brother was the bar manager, and we had a foreman, Dave. I arrived late after the season started, but they needed help once school was out, when the camp was regularly full. The two Scotsmen could easily have been from the Glasgow underworld. They told us to take the drinks offered us as tips by showing the bottle we planned to drink later to the customer. The money went into the cash register and we never saw it again. We were allocated one beer at lunch and another when we finished our shift at eleven o' clock. Well it did not need a Wall Street economist to work out who made money out of that deal, and I noticed my fellow workers started keeping their tips. If what they did was in plain sight to me, I knew it was only a matter of time before the brothers would notice as well. I called a meeting.

The atmosphere was tense when I informed them what I knew. I did not have much time to convince them I was not a rat, but a street-smart educated man, who could help cover our tracks. We weren't really stealing, I said, merely recovering what was ours. I told them they would be discovered if they carried on as they were.

We decided on an amount, and when we would take it. The time when we were under the least surveillance was the first hour of the evening during bingo. Not many customers came to the bar. The brothers did not start to watch us until the heavy traffic started. Even though it was risky, because only the 'float' was in the cash register, we took a pound note from each register twice during bingo. We squeezed it tightly in our hands, so the patron could not see, and immediately went out to the kitchen and hid it in our socks, or wherever we felt it would be safe. We then had the whole night to work that money off each of the cash registers, so it would go unnoticed. We waited until it was busy, then walked to a register away from the customer's view to ring up a lower amount. I also told my partners that when we restocked and counted the sales, to line the bottles six deep, but to place five in every third line. As we counted them out it would be six, twelve, eighteen, and so on.

The two Scotsmen were not the brightest characters, and I think most of their intimidating tactics were for show. However, it was not wise to cross them. My fellow barmen were seasonal workers, drifters, they had no plan for their future. Some of them had been in trouble with the law, they had no idea where they would be in a year or two. I was different because I had a plan. I think they respected me because I was going to college.

The worker's chalets were separated by gender and men were not allowed near the women's quarters. Of course, we were going to fraternize, but we needed to be careful not to get caught, especially since there was a security guard called 'Old Tom' whose main function was to be visible for the campers. Tom prided himself on keeping the men and the women who worked at the camp in their segregated areas.

One night one of our kitchen workers took exception to being found in a women's chalet. He beat up the security guard. Old Tom was at least seventy years old. Many of us were gathered in a chalet when the perpetrator joined us, looking scared. He had heard the two Scots brothers were after him. Suddenly the door burst open and the eldest of the two brothers dragged our co-worker out.

After he gave him a severe beating, the manager immediately fired the worker. What shocked me was I thought the elder Scots brother was at least seventy years old. It reminded me that what I heard about the east end of London was probably very similar to Glasgow. I needed to make sure I had a better future, so I didn't have to work in places like this again.

SIXTH FORM.

I received the O level results in the summer after school let out, so I completely surprised my schoolmates when I showed up for the first day of sixth form. I was the center of attention, with everybody congratulating me as if I had achieved something incredible, when in fact all the others had passed seven, eight or even nine O levels.

Some of the teachers did not know how to handle it. Mr. Poulter, my outstanding history teacher, was delighted. He liked my writing style but warned me not everyone would. Other teachers smiled as if something very good had happened, but they were also wary, because at the end of my fifth year I had still not demonstrated beyond a doubt I was ready to take school seriously.

I felt ecstatic because it meant I had two more years of playing football. I had demonstrated as a fifth year I was good enough for the first team. I was clearly a useful addition in what was a very good high school team. An interesting situation manifested itself in our winter practices, which took place in the gym. I discovered that playing on a hard service in the gym with a soft ball, and so called 'slippers' on my feet, I was a much better player than on grass. In fact, it became a little embarrassing for the older boys.

As a fifth year I played quite a bit on the first team, but I was not a regular selection in what was an outstanding high school team. However, at practices in the gym I handled the small ball better than anybody. I had a knack for using the walls to pass it to myself, I could turn and accelerate much better on a hard floor. I sensed the embarrassment in the gym when we selected teams. Three or four captains from the older boys took turns to choose teams for three a side soccer. It was a strange moment. I could tell they wanted to pick me because I was better than their older friends. They wanted to win, and they knew if they did not pick me the next captain might.

They seemed to always lower their heads and mumble out my name. They were embarrassed. I did not care. I sometimes felt like George Best must have felt as I ran amuck, scoring at will. I was nowhere near the same on grass. How odd! The ball was slower on grass, unfortunately so was I.

SCHOOL UNIFORMS.

The concept of school uniforms is complex. It originated with the public schools like Eton and Harrow as something to be proud of. Much later many English secondary schools required uniforms, so the poorer children would not be recognized by their shabby clothing. If all children wore the same clothes it was supposed to minimize the social class difference. However, it really did not matter. The more affluent always wore cleaner clothes that fit, and the poor children often wore older ill-fitting clothes.

Monteagle did not require uniforms, but when I started at Barking Abbey, I was required to wear a green blazer, grey trousers, and a school tie. We had to buy this from one certain shop, where they also sewed on the required badge, in the color of one's house assignment. This was not cheap. My mother paid for my first blazer when I was eleven years old.

The problem is I started to grow. We could not afford a new blazer, so I continued to wear the same one which clearly was too small, and it also showed real signs of wear. I also should admit I was not the best at taking care of my clothes. Playground football was my top priority. Since I was the youngest it was incumbent of me to put my blazer down to mark one side of a playground goal.

When it was time for a new blazer it was down to me and the secondhand market within the student body. There were plenty of green blazers available over the years, so finding one with the right color badge was not that difficult. In the sixth form, students wore different blazers. They had stripes and were very distinctive. They were also extremely expensive, and of course my mother refused to pay for mine. There was a problem with the secondhand market in sixth form because there were fewer blazers to pick from. When anybody purchased a new blazer, he would tell the shop the color of his badge, because it represented his house. Now if you found a graduating student willing to sell, there was a three to one chance the blazer would have the right color badge, because there were four houses.

I was a smaller boy, so it was difficult enough for me to find somebody my size willing to sell me his blazer. When I finally found one it had the red badge of Clugny House. I belonged to Citeaux House which had a yellow badge. This did not bother me as I had seen other boys do this. But it was a little confusing when a boy we did not know very well played for his house in sports, and the color we saw on his blazer during school time was different. The blazer I found was cheaper, a little big, had the wrong color badge and at first was no real problem.

It took a year for my blazer to become a problem when I was elected house captain by the younger boys. I was the obvious choice because of my proven athletic ability. It must have seemed strange to the younger boys at house meetings as they looked up at their captain, wondering why his blazer had a red badge, when almost everybody else had a yellow one. I soon learned to take off my blazer at house meetings.

Another problem was far more serious. I lived in Dagenham and now took the bus to school. Previously, my green blazer was like many others. I blended in and did not attract attention.

The sixth form blazer was very different. I did not want to risk walking to the bus stop wearing a very loud red and blue striped blazer. It was an invitation to the secondary modern kids to assault me. I owned a very light plastic raincoat which covered my stripes. On some summer days when it was very hot, I still walked to the bus stop with my raincoat on.

PROBLEMS IN SIXTH FORM.

Sixth form should have been my salvation. My problem was teachers like Emma and Taffy had brought out the rebel in me. I know I was immature not to seize my opportunity, but to be honest, I only stayed on at school to play football, and to hang out with my friends. My other Dagenham friends had all gone off to work.

I still got in trouble with Frank the headmaster, mostly for being late with homework and late for school. I had accumulated bad conduct marks which turned into detentions. I think Frank didn't know what to do with me. Caning had not worked, so he produced the trump card. He banned me from sports. This hurt. I tried harder and began to act in a more mature manner. In the spring of my lower sixth an odd thing happened.

The school used lower sixth boys as prefects when the upper sixth took exams. This also served as a trial run for selecting new upper sixth prefects. I was surprised to be selected and I can guess why. This was a school that valued tradition.

The staff realized I was probably going to captain the football team the next year. It was also highly likely that I would be elected house captain, because a captain was chosen by a student vote. They usually selected the best athlete to lead them in inter house sports. I think the staff knew it would be strange for the football captain, and the boy most likely to be voted house captain, to not be a prefect.

Unfortunately, I did not take advantage of their faith. The prefect's main job was to be responsible for the supervision of a younger class, waiting in line outside a classroom after recess. It must have been noticed I sometimes sprinted in late from the playground football game. When I did reach the upper sixth, I was not selected as a prefect.

The upper sixth gave me the chance to finally redeem myself. Although most of those who stayed on in sixth form chose three A level subjects to study, I took two. I think many teachers were surprised by my O level results and thought it might have been a fluke. I studied history and geography. In history I had an excellent teacher Mr. Poulter; in geography, for my sins, I had 'Taffy.' They were such a contrast. Poulter liked my writing style, which was brief and to the point. Taffy did not like me, and the rest of the class implored me not to goad him.

Taffy was a poor teacher, who quite simply read to us from a book. He also could not stay focused on his subject without bringing up something happening in the news, and his opinion of it. It was as if somebody was feeding me treats. I loved to argue with him. I could easily bait him, and I was stubborn. My classmates, mainly intelligent girls, begged me to stop. My excuse was we could all read the book he was reading to us.

Once again we sat mock exams, this time for A levels. I failed geography (I wonder why) but I passed history. I dropped geography. I spent my time writing answers to former history A level papers in my inimitable style, receiving good marks and comments from Mr. Poulter.

I was shocked when I failed A level history, and so was Mr. Poulter. My history failure completely indicted the validity of the exam system. It could well have been my writing style. Both O levels and A levels are marked by outside teachers during their summer break. Names are not printed on the exams they read, so they could not know who wrote the paper, or where they came from. I am not saying I was entitled to pass, but next year when I was working, I applied to retake my history A level. The problem was I was too busy to study for it.

The exam paper had three parts: English, European, and Roman history. I had left school, so I traveled into London on three separate days to take the exam. After the first two days, I was convinced I had made a mistake. I had not studied, so I did not perform anywhere near my previous level. I decided it was a waste of my time to go and write the third paper. Roman history was my weakest subject. I proceeded to just sit at home and feel bad. However, I was not a quitter. I decided to set off for the exam, even though I knew I would arrive late. I would do what I could but was convinced it would not be good enough.

Later I received notification I had passed my history A level. How could it be? It seems to me outcomes were far too dependent on *which* teachers did the marking. Clearly in my first attempt, the one I studied hard for, my paper was marked by somebody who did not like my writing style. My much weaker second attempt must have been marked by somebody who was very forgiving of my lack of content, but clearly liked my style.

It is an indictment of the system if you ask me, but I felt happy. I remember reading Trevor Brooking's book where he comments on a similar experience.

COULD I ATTEND COLLEGE?

During my time in sixth form I had formed a good relationship with Ron Gould, the physical education teacher. He, like me, was somewhat of a fish out of water. He originated from the north of England and spoke with a strong northern accent, which we made fun of, behind his back of course. The academic teachers looked down on him, as they also did with the teachers of art and craft and other non-academic subjects. Ron did not care. He was his own man. He drove a Mercedes, the most expensive car in the parking lot. He was married to a night club singer, who was clearly the person bringing in the money at his house.

Ron was a typical ageing physical education teacher. He arrived late, gave us a ball, sent us out to the fields, and showed up at the end to bring us in. He felt no pressure. The school did not care about non-academic subjects.

I talked to him a lot about how I could become a teacher of physical education. Ron took a real interest. He advised me to apply to the top physical education colleges, known as *wing* colleges. He urged me to apply to the college he had attended, Carnegie College in Yorkshire. I applied to other wing colleges as well.

Of course, applications were made with the expectations of passing A level exams. Students would be interviewed and given conditional acceptance, which was dependent on passing two A levels with grades of C or above. Many of my classmates applied to more academic universities, where two A's and a B might be the acceptance formula.

The letter offering me an interview at Carnegie informed me I needed to take a practical exam, involving vaulting over a vaulting horse, and doing a floor exercise. Things had changed since Ron was at Carnegie.

Colleges had started specializing, and they looked for talented students who could help them in competition. Carnegie specialized in gymnastics, hence the test. I was happy to vault, but I had never been taught any form of gymnastic floor work. Ron said, "Just do a forward roll and your best vault, it is not that important." Carnegie did not offer me a place.

Other colleges I interviewed with did not require any such performance, but I applied to the best. Once I dropped my geography A level, I knew the colleges I applied to were off limits. There were plenty of other colleges that my name would be sent to if I did not make it, but it was getting late in the process.

Then of all things, Frank Young was following my progress, or lack of it. My headmaster admitted to me in one of our conversations, quite probably after a caning, that he liked me. I think he knew about the difficulty

I had at home, compared to the other boys at his school. He called me into his office for quite possibly the first time where I was not in trouble. He told me a local school, 'Gearies Boys School', wanted a graduating sixth former to teach at their school as an assistant for a year. The pay was good for somebody starting out. I agreed to interview.

It was so easy to say yes to this opportunity. I would satisfy my mother by finally bringing home some real money, not just a meagre contribution. I could reapply to lesser colleges where my experience would override my problem of having no A levels, although one would come later. The position required some classroom teaching, but I would spend most of my time assisting the physical education teacher.

LEARNING MY TRADE.

I forget my official title, but in 1968 I was hired as an assistant teacher, with responsibility for teaching some classes for other teachers, to ease their workload. I helped with history, geography, and physical education.

At first, I only taught with a regular teacher present in the classroom or the gym. In the classroom, the regular teacher sat at the back, marking books. I flourished at Gearies, to the extent that it was not long before the history and geography teachers left the room. They believed I could handle the situation.

The physical education teacher Bryn Jones and I became good friends. We divided the class and I taught half. I really enjoyed myself, and it confirmed to me that I wanted to pursue teacher training at college, and major in physical education.

Gearies was an all-boys school and not an easy school to teach in. Even though it bordered the suburb of Ilford, a town predominantly middle class, it had in the catchment area a 'Doctor Barnados' home, an orphanage. The boys from the orphanage attended the school. Many could be difficult, but most of the time they appreciated the attention given to them. At times, they really tested the teachers. The experience provided me with valuable training before going to college.

Our staff had a strong welsh contingent. There was a joke that the welsh either taught or went down into the mines. I can remember Bryn, Alf, Lynn, and Mike, and I became friends with all of them. There was a small pool table in the middle of our staff room, which was in use all the time. We also met at a pub most Friday evenings, where we played snooker on a full-size table.

Alf was older and was a strong disciplinarian. When I walked into his classroom there was absolute silence, with the boys all working from their math books. Lynn was a tall handsome man with an eye for the women. Mike was the enigma. He was always negative. He complained about the boys, the head, the other staff. I could only imagine the negativity in his classroom. There was an incident later in the year, when a class he constantly berated to us, turned on him. Apparently, it started with one student slowly banging a desk lid and others joined in. They must have conspired beforehand because even though he shouted with threats of punishment at them, they continued until he left the room. It was near the end of the year and I heard Mike subsequently left the school.

I worked mostly with Bryn Jones. He and I became good friends. I had to take two buses to get to work. Soon he picked me up at the second bus stop in the morning and would drop me there at night. After the pub on a Friday night he took me all the way home. A former gymnast he worked hard with boys after school to develop an interest in competitive gymnastics. I also benefitted from his expertise. What amused me was had I interviewed at Carnegie College during my spell at this school, I would have performed a much better vault, plus a decent floor exercise.

Of course, they did not give me the best and the brightest to teach. I think the fact my teachers initially stayed in the classroom gave me time to establish my credibility with the class. I felt very comfortable, but my real love was teaching physical education. I began to look for colleges to apply to, so I could become a qualified physical education teacher.

I did not apply to any of the colleges I had applied to the year before. Clearly Ron's advice was not good, although I do not blame him. Times had changed. I also know he wanted the best for me. After a few rejections, it came down to two possibilities. A college south of London and one in Manchester in northern England.

I interviewed at both and settled on Didsbury College in Manchester, mainly because they accepted me. I accepted before I heard from the other college. I was worried they might change their minds.

I found out later Didsbury was expanding their enrollment. One of my future friends arrived a week late, after being accepted earlier that same week. Many of my friends told similar stories. They had been turned down at other colleges and grabbed the offer from Didsbury College immediately. They found a college willing to accept them.

PART TWO,
COLLEGE AND TEACHING.

FOOTBALL IN COLLEGE.

College of course is a daunting experience as one sets off into the unknown. I was almost twenty years old. I remember the introductory meeting, where I assumed everybody was in the same boat. I started talking to the person sitting next to me. We now know Ken Walters as 'Walt.' He remains a good friend. That night we both left the meeting and walked into Didsbury village to drink a beer.

We had a couple of things in common, we both majored in physical education and wanted to play on the football team. We were housed in Royal Ford Hall, where we mingled with other first year PE majors, who were also keen to try out for football.

We discovered a couple of things at the tryouts. The large first year class possessed some very good football players. The older third year boys welcomed us. We were going to improve the team. The second years were worried. They played an extremely physical brand of football. To be honest they played dirty in the tryouts. The first years demanded a meeting to find out why, but the other team members thought we were babies. I was not selected for the first team, so I settled in the second team for the entire year. Many of my newfound friends made the first team and our two teams travelled together. The first team was very good. I was not a physical player and relied on my good passing skills, plus my ability to score goals from a midfield position.

At Didsbury everybody trained to become teachers. Consequently, students had to give up training and playing for the football team when they were involved with 'teaching practice' in local schools. During a time when our older players were absent from our team for this reason, one of our greatest accomplishments happened.

We played at St. Johns College in York. They were the reigning national champions and had not lost in almost two years. With the senior class missing, no less than nine first year players suited up for the first team. I was not among them. It would take me two years to make the first team. I was on the second team playing against the St. Johns second team on an adjacent field. Our game finished about ten minutes before the first team game.

We sensed something was happening, so we went over to the field where the two first teams were playing. We asked the score and one of our players yelled out, "It is 3-1 for us." The St. Johns team were camped in our half and were totally dominating, trying their best to score. Didsbury finally broke out of defense and on a fast counter-attack Walt scored. The game was over, we had beaten the national champions.

It was common practice to dine with the other team, which we did, and then go to their college bar for a few drinks. This time we wanted to celebrate, so after hoisting a few with the opposition, we headed out to a pub for a few more before the ride home. After those 'few' drinks we came outside, and somebody saw the famous walls of medieval York castle. We climbed the walls and sang as loud as we could, before singing all the way home on a three-hour bus ride.

Football mattered to me and I worked hard to improve. The team changed over the years. Some players who started on the first team could not handle being left out of the team and quit. I stayed the course and became first team captain in my third year.

COLLEGE OF EDUCATION.

Didsbury was called a College of Education. It was a new term for the old title 'Teacher Training College.'

I struggled at college from the beginning. I knew I had a huge advantage over my fellow students, because I had already taught for a year. However, I had not studied during that year. In trying to reapply myself I encountered another disadvantage. As well as not going through the discipline of reading, studying and writing homework exercises for a year, I was also taking classes I did not choose.

During my last two years at high school I chose my subjects, history and geography, subjects which interested me. I also had a light load and plenty of time to apply myself. In my new environment, I was required to take courses in the psychology, philosophy and history of education. These subjects were taught by lecturers who may have been qualified, but who were limited in their ability to either make their subjects interesting or appealing in any way. I suspected these lecturers had only climbed the ladder of education to gain qualifications. We soon learned they either taught in areas where middle class children would pay attention, or they did not teach at all.

When we were sent into schools for our teaching practice, we were not instructed in the art of how to keep a class fully attentive. In fact, we all learned a phrase from older students that was paramount at the time. "Teachers who cannot teach, teach teachers." I remember being appalled by the lack of interest shown by George Grime one of our physical education lecturers. He ran our course of football, and he displayed a badge on his shirt showing the highest qualification in football coaching.

As I said, our first-year class was a very talented class of football players. We would have relished and benefitted from good coaching. The winning result we achieved at St. Johns came without the services of our third-year players, who were student teaching. Remember not only were nine players first years, we also had quite a few first-year players in the second team. A lecturer with the highest coaching qualifications should have salivated over the chance to coach such a young team. It could have been a project over three years with a goal; a national championship. After all we had demonstrated we had the ability.

We knew he was not coaching anywhere else at the time. He epitomized most of the college lecturers we encountered at school. They aspired to a better paying job that required less work.

There were a couple of exceptions, lecturers who taught track and field, Mr. Harper, and rugby, Mr. Quinn. They were excellent and knew their stuff, whereas in the theory of education sessions we rarely experienced anybody who excited, interested, or challenged us. The two leading lights, Mr. Kenyon and Mr. Lee, heads of the department if you like, were a joke.

I wondered, given my recent classroom teaching experience how these people could possibly keep the children's attention in anything, because they certainly did not make our experience interesting. It is quite possible that some of these lecturers found teaching appealing because of the frequent semester breaks and school vacations. However, they did not realize how much energy went into being a good teacher, one who excited and inspired the children.

I remember one attempt to supposedly modernize what we did. A female lecturer came to teach us 'dance.' This was part of the curriculum, a modern approach to body awareness and movement, described by one source as:

'The educational gymnastics component seeks to provide students with an understanding and aesthetic appreciation of artistic and expressive movement. Skills learnt are never an end in themselves but add to an individual's movement vocabulary, enabling a response to open-ended tasks. The process of educational gymnastics emphasizes affective, cognitive and psychomotor development. Sequencing is a strategy to be used continuously from the very beginning to harness the various skills and content of the syllabus. Group work and partner interaction are encouraged, so that students work cooperatively and support each other to create novel responses to tasks that may often be beyond their individual physical limits and abilities.'

The attempt to teach this to a bunch of male college students was farcical. There were about thirty of us, teenagers in their first year of college. We were asked to *'feel'* the music, and have our bodies move accordingly.

Given my year of classroom teaching experience one of my peers later asked me whether using this dance teaching theory would be effective. I told them categorically not to try this with secondary boys in a gymnasium. If it was in the inner city, it would have been farcical. It might have worked at a school in a more affluent area, where discipline could have been a little easier. The female lecturer was appalled when one of our students, Mike Bell, burst into hysterical laughter during the class, and she was forced to abandon the project. Mr. Kenyon, who had invited her, was annoyed. It was his decision to introduce this new form of teaching gymnastics.

My criticism is a little biased because I had taught a year at a school where the head of the physical education department was a former college gymnast. He focused on competitive gymnastics. With him I learned a great deal and I improved my own gymnastic ability. This earned me the respect of my college class.

There were times in my first year I was convinced I would not complete the year. The boring theory lectures, and the assignments associated with them, were a million miles away from the *'chalk face'* as I called it. The place where the teacher stood in front of a class with chalk in hand, teaching young people and deriving infinite pleasure from watching them learn. I was so glad I had experienced that pleasure, it kept me going.

I persevered through two terms of lectures and looked forward to the third term, when we would go out into the city to a school for our teaching practice. We were expected to teach both primary, age seven through eleven, and secondary, age eleven through sixteen. To me it was the most important part of my education.

When the time came, I was excited to find out I would begin my first teaching practice at a primary school in Oldham. My experience had been with secondary education, boys age eleven to sixteen. I was to teach a mixed class of boys and girls who were nine or ten years old, and it was just classroom teaching.

TEACHING PRACTICE.

Oldham, a suburb of Manchester, was famous for cotton mills and factories epitomizing the 'Industrial Revolution.' We all got up very early in the morning to ride the bus taking Didsbury College students to various suburbs. Our bus ride was not a happy one. When we received our assignments, we understood we would be teaching in a small industrial town inhabited predominantly by factory workers. We could identify the children as working class by their shabby attire. I knew how they felt because that was my history.

Oldham.

My year of experience at 'Gearies' was invaluable. I knew I could control a class of boys who were ten years old, because my previous experience was with older, probably more difficult boys. However, this class had girls.

Our only interaction with girls, or women as we knew them in college, was the farcical 'educational gymnastics' attempt I mentioned earlier. I had no experience teaching the other gender, but these girls were not too difficult. I taught all different subjects because it was a primary school, but I really looked forward to the physical education class. To my total surprise we did not have a gymnasium or a changing room. I taught the class in the main hall.

The children did not change into different clothes, so I was asking them to roll around on the floor in their school clothes. Trying to teach educational gymnastics in such a setting was virtually impossible. When the girls were asked to perform some of the movements we had been taught in educational gymnastics at college, it meant their skirt would fall over their head. It was quite clear this would not work.

I found out their class teacher just played games during gym class. However, I expected to be graded by a visiting physical education lecturer on what he had taught his students to teach. I should not have worried. Our lecturers did not travel to the poorer areas, they visited schools in the nearby and more affluent suburbs. We learned of this from our older residents at college, so it was not a problem. I imagine I was graded by my classroom teacher at Oldham and I know I received a good grade. Nobody from my college of education came to watch me.

Not being evaluated by a physical education instructor was very disappointing considering this was my chosen vocation. In some ways it was good, as I was evaluated by a real teacher. The most interesting part of my first teaching practice was the way my friends came to me for advice. They all knew I had previous experience, so I was surrounded on the bus ride home, and often called upon in the residence halls. It did not take long for my fellow students to realize our lecturers had not prepared us for teaching at ninety per cent of the schools in the country. We also learned the theory had little practical application. We learned by experience, and I was lucky because I had more than my peers.

A College of Education was a three-year experience with a teaching practice component each year. To obtain a 'Bachelor of Education' degree required an extra year, something I not only did not want, but could not afford. The first teaching practice was four weeks, followed by five weeks in the second year and seven in the third.

It was now the end of my first year at college. I did not have good grades, but I did have a good grade in the 'practice of education'. I had made some very good friends, I had enjoyed football, but we left to go home for the summer holidays, which were not holidays for me.

To continue to attend college it was necessary for me to make a lot of money during the summer vacation. I was very lucky in that regard. I had found ways and means of financing my future.

I returned to college for my second year with great anticipation, mostly because it meant reuniting with my friends. We were all eager to talk about the summer, as in those days every student was expected to work. I also felt I could do better academically because I could choose more of my classes. I still needed to take the theory classes, which were not only boring but contained nothing that would help me in my chosen career. I really struggled with the philosophy of education. I could not fathom how this would help me.

The second year meant teaching practice was in a secondary school, my preferred area of expertise. When I found out my assignment was in a suburb of Manchester called Wythenshawe, I was a little concerned. It was not an affluent suburb and had a reputation for being a rough area. It also began to dawn on most of my friends that there was some favoritism regarding our assignments. Some of our fellow students had more affinity with the lecturers. It seemed they received better assignments, teaching in middle class areas. Many of these schools were near the college campus. This was not only advantageous to these students, but it made travel to do evaluations easier for the lecturers.

My teaching practice was difficult, but I survived, and I received a good grade. There were criticisms from my supervising physical education lecturer, who watched one of my classes. He had obviously never taught in such an area. He may well have had only slightly more experience than me. We had all learned that the experience of teaching was proving far more valuable than anything we were being taught in college.

In the summer after my second year I earned enough money at the swimming pool, with all the overtime, to continue my third and last year at college, which was a strange year. Some friends rented a beautiful apartment which had five bedrooms. They stayed in Manchester over the summer and saved a place for me. There were nine of us, including two older working friends. We were scheduled to take our final and most important teaching practice almost immediately after returning to college. Once again, I was disappointed by the location of my school, as were my roommates with theirs.

However, I had a bigger problem. My athlete's foot had worsened considerably. My feet had completely shed the old skin. The new skin was very tender. I very carefully followed my doctor's advice.

The problem reared its ugly head when I visited my assigned school. The head of department was only too pleased to show me around. Many teachers enjoyed having students on teaching practice. It meant they had less to do. This teacher was so proud that his school had its own swimming pool, an unusual feature at the time. When he informed me over half my lessons would be conducted in the pool. I was devastated.

I immediately arranged to see my advisor. I did not think they would do anything, so I thought I must drop out of college, to make them understand the gravity of my situation. A swimming pool was the root of my problem. I was expected to walk around barefoot. I asked to be moved to a different school for obvious reasons. I really did not want to teach any lessons in a pool with my feet in such poor condition. There was a distinct possibility my condition could deteriorate.

There was a new lecturer, Peter Harper, who had moved to our college after teaching some years at a respected grammar school nearby, which typically did not take our students. It was Cheadle Hulme Grammar School.

He asked the school if they would take me, and they agreed. I was delighted, but my friends were not. They thought I had sought out special treatment. The problem was exacerbated by the fact their assigned schools were not anywhere near as good as mine. They had to travel further and teach in rougher schools. They let me know it, comparing me to others in our class, who were friendly with the lecturers.

However, I was undeterred. I fired back that they could not possibly understand my situation. Surely, they must have seen my feet. I was boiling my socks daily and constantly putting cream on my feet to keep the fungus away.

I must be honest though my assignment at Cheadle Hulme School was much easier. I taught middle class children who wanted to be taught. The head of the physical education department was an excellent teacher. I respected the way he ran his program and I learned a great deal from him. I received a commendation for my teaching practice when it was over.

Cheadle Hulme School.

We were all ready to finish and leave college when a strange thing happened. The head of the physical education department at Cheadle Hulme School needed knee surgery, so he called the college and asked if I was available. The school was prepared to pay me. The college granted the request providing that I made up the work I would miss. I really enjoyed teaching and had made a strong friendship with the head of department. There was a bonus for the boys too.

Generally, a school philosophy on the games being taught in physical education classes was biased toward either rugby or football. Cheadle Hulme was a rugby school, but my supervisor wanted me to teach the boys football. It was another reason I admired him, as many others would not have been as flexible.

I really enjoyed this experience and the money also helped enormously.

MY FIRST TEACHING ASSIGNMENT.

The education system in the whole country in the early 1970's was changing. The elitist system I benefitted from, was being overhauled. Three types of schools, the grammar, technical high and secondary modern schools, were merging into comprehensive schools. I applied to teach at a school that was halfway through the process when looking for my first job.

I was accepted for the post of assistant teacher in the physical education department at Salford Grammar Technical School. The city of Salford was a small city situated alongside the larger city Manchester, about two hundred miles north of London.

It was most definitely one of the best jobs around. I am sure it was the references from Cheadle Hulme School, the school I had helped during my final year at college, that really proved useful. I also had a commendation in the practice of teaching, which in my opinion counted more than any commendations in academic work.

I was the third member of the physical education department of the largest school in Salford, and it proved to be a very interesting couple of years. The two merging schools were separated by playing fields. The grammar school was the only one of its kind in Salford. It of course over time had attracted some very qualified teachers.

In the amalgamation, the head of department positions were almost all awarded to the teachers at the grammar school, while the technical high teachers were offered other staff positions. To demonstrate some equality, the technical high school department heads were awarded similar positions in the lesser academic subjects. This was true of the physical education department which I joined.

The head of department was Bob Marsden, who held the same position at the technical high school. The second member was Roy Lilleyman who had headed the grammar school department. They had worked together for two years when I arrived.

These two men could not have been more different. I was assigned to the old grammar school side with Roy. I was told to observe how both men taught whenever possible, which I did. Roy was an excellent teacher, who was very interested in the progress of the pupils. He was heavily involved in after school activities. I became good friends with Roy, and it was obvious he felt let down about not being given the head of department position.

Bob had a military background and it showed. He lined his pupils up under corresponding numbers on the wall of the gym and took attendance in case boys missed class. He was always deliberately late. He tried to create the kind of military environment of an officer arriving to address his men. Bob did not participate in any after school activities.

Each school had one office in the gym, so I needed some office space. Bob told me to make an office on the balcony above the gym using large cupboards as the perimeter. The balcony was unused other than for storage. It was dirty because the custodians did not clean storage areas very thoroughly. Bob told me to use students who forgot their gym kit to clean it, apparently without supervising them. It was typical Bob. By the time we sorted all this out the class time was shortened.

I ignored Bob. I did not need an office, and I wanted to teach these enthusiastic young boys. My students quickly responded. They ran to my gym class and changed very quickly. Bob lectured me on a couple of occasions, and I ignored him. He ordered me to paint the numbers on the gym wall, which I did. Unfortunately, my painting expertise was so poor the finished product looked awful. Even so, we still did not use his ridiculous system.

It is worth noting the dilemma facing all physical education teachers. It is very much a young person's vocation. We were all warned about needing to change teaching positions as we aged, but when you are young and enthusiastic you cast these thoughts aside. I replaced a teacher, Keith Livesley, who now taught history. Most physical education teachers moved into the classroom in their late thirties.

I was a very enthusiastic young teacher. Roy was an exception but was approaching the time when he might have to change. Bob earned a high salary as a head of department. This made a lateral move difficult, particularly since he did not exhibit any skills to endear him to any other head of department position.

I was handed the football coaching assignment of the first team. These were the oldest boys. The schedule however was a problem. The school had inherited the traditional grammar school schedule. It was no wonder other teachers did not want to coach the older boys. They were over matched against schools from the larger city, Manchester. The technical high school however had played teams from the smaller schools in Salford.

In the merger the younger teams were competitive with the grammar school schedule they played on a Saturday, and they dominated when playing the smaller Salford schools midweek. It would change in two years. The Greater Manchester area would undergo a major teaching theory revision, the introduction of comprehensive education. I would also benefit from the change and secure a Head of Department job at a smaller school.

I know the boys really appreciated the coaching, as up and until then they had not received any from a qualified soccer coach. The teachers who ran the teams were volunteers with no coaching background.

It was a different story with basketball. The catchment area, the area immediately around the school from where the school derived their pupils, was the more affluent part of Salford. This meant the boys attending the school were generally bigger and certainly more disciplined. I really wanted to take a young team and coach them at basketball. My history with the sport was limited. Until I attended college, I had played very little.

When I attended college, I played soccer with my circle of friends from my physical education group. When basketball started, they all tried out. I would go watch them rather than sit home alone. The coach was excellent and a local physical education teacher. He would invite me to be a practice player from time to time. I quickly found out one did not need excellent skills to play defense. By the end of my first year I played on the college second team. We also played pick-up basketball in our free time.

The basketball coach, Bill Beswick, laid out an excellent curriculum which I brought with me into teaching. I took a young team and we played against the smaller schools in the area. It was clear from the start our boys were bigger, more skilled, and had the discipline to run an offense and play defense.

There were no officials assigned to our games. Both coaches officiated. I noticed early on that other coaches watched our games, and quickly found out it was *'us against them'*. They resented the size of our school and the size and ability of our players. They had scouted us and were ready for plays we ran because they had communicated with each other. I did not mind, and I understood why they would do this, as they deemed it unfair. They may have done this with the previous coaches, however in one of the first games I experienced something that made me angry.

Our tallest player Mike was a good shooter, but not aggressive in the slightest, and we accepted he did not defend very well. In an early game the opposing coach whistled Mike for three fouls in the first ten minutes. I was appalled. After a time out, with Mike sitting on the bench, I started calling fouls on their best player. I stared at the coach after I blew the whistle. It was obvious, if we carried on doing this then both of each team's best players would not finish the game. We won the game and I confronted Tony Moore the coach afterwards. He backed down, and strangely enough we ended up becoming good friends over the years.

I understand now how frustrating it must have been for all the smaller schools in the area to go against a much larger school. Results were obviously good for us, but we were not responsible for the disparity in the school system. What became incredibly interesting was the situation I encountered a couple of years down the road. I coached at a different school, going up against my old school where I experienced the same disadvantage from the other side.

A SOCIAL EDUCATION.

As I said, the coach Tony and I became friends. He asked if I wanted to earn some extra money by working, as he did, for a small company that collected rent from people who leased slot televisions. My young teacher's salary was not very substantial, and it reinforced my opinion that authorities kept teacher's salaries low to avoid people coming into the profession just for the money.

Tony introduced me to the company owner. He rented second-hand televisions to low income clientele by attaching a small box to the back of the television into which a renter could deposit coins to make the television work. A collector came to empty the boxes and they wanted me to be one.

What seemed to be a straightforward collection job did have drawbacks. Sometimes a collector needed to repossess a television, if there was not enough money in the box. Most of the repossessions were prompted because renters broke into the boxes when they were short of cash. I took the job. I earned a small percentage of the collection money, plus a repossession fee if necessary.

About sixty to seventy per cent of the customers gave me no problems. They were glad to see me, because after I emptied the box and had taken the amount for the rent, I returned the remaining coins. This sometimes amounted to two or three pounds, but the main reason for this business was to give people of less means a chance to have a television set. The other twenty to thirty per cent presented difficulties. The renters did not have the money. They had no problem breaking into the boxes and taking the cash. Dave, the owner of the company, said he would let them continue to rent if they paid cash on the spot. Most people did not have the cash, so I repossessed the televisions.

I drove a small van, and in the evening when I finished my rounds, I sometimes had two or three televisions in the back. Dave was happy I did the difficult repossession job but of course he lost money with every repo. These customers immediately called another company to start again. Dave even listened to them if they wanted to rent from him again.

He asked me to keep a regular route and collect on the same day each week. He reasoned if they knew I was coming, the customers would either put the money back, or at least would be ready to pay. I had a problem with collecting on the same day of the week. These were tough neighborhoods.

If I kept to a regular route, I could become a target for a thief or a mugger. There was also the problem of customers simply not answering their doors, because they knew it was me. This meant coming back.

Sometimes I knocked on so many unanswered doors that I had to arrange another night to collect. I did not want that.

The conditions in some of the houses appalled me. Small children crawled on floors filthy with garbage. I have always wondered why we teach subjects like algebra to large numbers of children who really need to be taught health and hygiene, or how to take care of a family when they are older.

When I look back, I cannot believe how dangerous this job was. I carried a cash bag in poor neighborhoods, known for crime. Since I mostly collected coins, I deposited them in the bag and kept them ready to use as a weapon if I was set upon. I was extremely vigilant and watched for anybody who looked suspicious. We all become wiser with age. The best solution, if threatened, would have been to just drop the cash and run. Luckily, I was never threatened. I only collected for a couple of years. The money helped, but I really wanted to earn promotion at my school, so I could give up collecting.

TIME FOR A CHANGE.

I have already said the life of a physical education teacher is short. We all believe as young entrants into the profession that it will never happen to us. We will not lose our enthusiasm as we age. However, it was easy to observe my predecessors. Their enthusiasm waned especially when faced with going outside in freezing weather to teach.

This continued when confronted with night after night of extracurricular activities, like games and practices followed by rush hour traffic. Other teachers were home by 4.00 as opposed to 6.30. It also meant giving up every Saturday morning. While other teachers enjoyed Saturday morning with their families, I would be sat on a bus going to another school for a game.

I learned from other physical education teachers that if you were not rewarded early for your extra work, it is likely the school did not care enough to keep you. It was important to know they wanted you to stay. Physical education teachers who became too old to face the daily grind posed an administrative problem. The problem of how to find them alternative places on the staff.

I started my teaching career when the comprehensive education movement was in full swing around the country. The Labour Party introduced this philosophic switch because they objected to the so called 'privileged' classes receiving a better education in the grammar schools; an education determined, as mine was, by the results of an exam at the age of eleven, called the eleven plus. Much larger comprehensive schools were created so that movement up and down, according to ability, could occur within the same school.

When I was offered the Salford Grammar Tech job, I remember one of the other candidates Chris Hetherington made a point of congratulating me. He and the other candidates were then asked to interview for another job in the district. He was later offered that job, and he accepted the position of head of department at Broughton Modern, one of the smaller schools in Salford. After two years he resigned, and the job was offered at a scale three level of responsibility.

Broughton Modern changed its' name to Broughton High School, a comprehensive school, and the scale three position was a promotion. I started teaching as all new teachers did as a scale one instructor. I asked for a scale two at my first school after two years and was denied. Scale two positions were mostly for assistants. Once a teacher advanced to scale three many of the positions were either assistants in large schools, or heads of department in small ones. There was a big difference.

What they did at Broughton Modern was take Chris, a first-year teacher, and put him in charge of the department. They saved money by keeping him on a scale one. It was a mistake. He struggled in a very difficult school, as I will explain later.

Money was poured into the comprehensive changeover and new positions were created. When I saw there was a head of department job at Broughton High School listed on a scale three, I was interested. First, it was more money, but it was also a chance to be the boss and make the decisions. I applied and was accepted. When Pat Partington the deputy head called me in after the interview to offer me the job, she joked, "I thought for a moment you had left." I did not understand the humor then, but I did later. Errol Davies, the teacher who helped the previous PE teacher, and who also applied for the head of department job, became my part time assistant. I really did not know what I was getting into. The difference between the two schools was enormous.

GAINING ACCEPTANCE.

At Broughton High I joined a staff who had been there a while. With the huge influx of promotion money some were happy, and some were disappointed. There was a staff camaraderie that I experienced later, but I was treated at first as an outsider. I had taken the job they thought belonged to one of their own and bringing me in was not a popular decision.

I thrived at the responsibility I was given and set about introducing a modern curriculum. A previous department head Les Proctor was now head of fifth year, and he offered me advice about how he did things. My assistant Errol Davies had previously applied for my job. I understood whatever I did would draw criticism, but I did not care. There was clearly a social life with this group, and an inner circle I needed to crack, but I did not participate at first, I was too busy. I was happy to be my own boss, and I began doing what I thought best to improve the department.

The immediate problem was the local education authority thought by changing the philosophy of the school they could make it better. However, if you wanted an example of why a school should never be built in a certain location, Broughton Modern was a prime example. Two very large buildings overshadowed our school, a prison and a brewery. A public house was directly across the street from the front entrance, and we bordered one of the worst neighborhoods in one of the worst cities in England. It was an awful location.

I was surprised the inner circle of teachers spent their lunch hour in a public house. I could not believe they would teach the second half of the day with alcohol on their breath. I found out later many of the student's parents regularly drank to extreme, so I suppose this made little difference.

The teachers did not invite me to join them for lunch at the pub. I would not have gone with them anyway. Lunch hours for a physical education teacher were for extracurricular activities. I ate lunch in the cafeteria and then went to the gymnasium, or the track, so interested pupils could receive some coaching in whatever sport was current.

However, I did want to fit in. When I heard the staff was going out for a social evening I asked for the location, so I could join them. I arrived to find nobody there. As I was leaving another one of the teachers came in and told me to follow him to the right location. I think this was their way of telling me what they thought of me, until somebody relented. At least one person thought I might be a decent chap. It was my first breakthrough.

I am a social animal. I have always been one. It did not take me long to gain acceptance and Errol was the prime mover. We quickly became friends, and the other teachers came around and accepted me virtually without exception.

I think I had the best work ethic. I gave up four lunch breaks and stayed four days after school to work with the better athletes. It was acceptable I was never going to be a lunch time drinker and my staff understood that.

The same time my position was created they created a corresponding one for girls. Sylvia Caulfield, the girl's physical education teacher, was very different than me. Although in the beginning she held a few lunch time activities she soon joined the social lunch crowd. She did not stay after school to run extra practices. The headmaster was not happy about this and it had major repercussions later. However, I did manage to convince her to send some of the older girls to me for an introduction to basketball.

HOW DIFFERENT COULD TEACHING BE?

This was to be my first encounter teaching girls at any level, other than a brief encounter on teaching practice.

In England at that time the most popular sport for girls was netball, a game fractured with stops and starts where the shooter was usually unopposed. The girls who came to me immediately liked basketball better, and they were very interested in playing more. I was impressed with their desire to learn, which was far greater than the boys. This experiment ended quickly when the girls did not willingly return to playing netball. I suspect my deteriorating relationship with Sylvia also had something to do with it.

As department heads Sylvia and I started on equal pay scales, but that did not last long. The headmaster was impressed I spent long hours after school and at lunch breaks with extra activities, while he knew she had joined the lunch crowd and headed home immediately after school. He knew the difference. The headmaster promoted me to Head of the Physical Education Department, which annoyed her intensely. I told Sylvia I would not interfere with what she did, but our relationship was tarnished.

The area around the school, as I explained, was not conducive in any way to an educational environment. The city recognized the fact and decided to build a huge sports center next door to the school. The center was very impressive, especially in a neighborhood which had no amenities. It was well staffed, and we were allowed total access for our physical education classes.

My goal was to try to make the center more attractive than the streets to the older students.

We offered what we called *'options'* to their PE classes. Along with the typical activities offered by any sports center I took interested students on rock climbing expeditions. Sometimes we went to indoor climbing walls, but we also drove out to local outcrops. These were not too far away but it often meant that students stayed very late after school hours, so I dropped them off at their house. This was when I witnessed the squalor of the local streets. I knew we teachers could positively impact their lives at school, but we were at the mercy of our student's home lives, and the life they found on the streets, where crime was accepted as a part of the community.

A new headmaster, Tony Blacas, was appointed after his predecessor retired. I really do not think he knew what he was getting into. He was given money to enact change amongst the staff. He asked me to take charge of the social welfare and discipline of the older students. It was promotion, and it offered me a way out of the physical education teacher's problem. What you do when you get older, and when going outside in the cold and damp becomes more demanding. Though it was promotion I enjoyed it far less than teaching.

My friend Walt took my place and I became his assistant, when I taught. This might have posed a problem, but we were good friends and had spent three years at college together, often sharing the same house or apartment.

I had a very flexible schedule and it allowed me to operate in my new position as a member of the senior management team. I could feel the resentment from the lunchtime crowd. I am sure they complained long and hard over their beers and said the jobs were going to the privileged, the ones who the headmaster liked. The headmaster knew about their lackadaisical attitudes and recognized me as a hardworking individual whom he could trust to do a good job. What I did not appreciate was the fact I was teaching less, and teaching was my first love.

CRIME AND PUNISHMENT.

One of the first problems I encountered in my new position was a backlash from the lunchtime crowd. If a boy, and most times it was a boy, misbehaved in class he was sent to me for punishment. This is how they perceived my job. Any good teacher knows it is far better to keep discipline in the classroom, rather than to abdicate responsibility to another. I did however accept there was an order of things and I was the disciplinarian.

If a teacher had disciplined a child, and the bad behavior continued, a higher punishment was needed. It was always my belief that a good teacher rarely if ever passed on behavioral problems, it was not the best way. There were several good teachers who at no time passed on their problems to me. However, some of the weaker teachers, often in the lunch group where I am sure I was not a favorite, would send a boy to me with the expectation that corporal punishment should be used.

Corporal punishment was still allowed in schools at the time. Any teacher could, if they so desired, use corporal punishment. It was generally expected it would be for a boy, as I cannot recall it ever being used on a girl. There were older teachers, where this had been normal discipline procedure for years, who took care of this themselves. Generally, the older better teachers had good discipline, so punishment of this kind was unnecessary.

When appropriate I used corporal punishment. There were times when a teacher sent a boy to me for caning where I failed to understand why the teacher had trouble with the boy. When the same boy was in my class, he never presented a problem. Only gradually did I understand that the weaker teachers were using me to do their dirty work, caning boys who I had no trouble with.

At first, I caned some of these boys, but I was quickly becoming tired of it. There were also boys to whom the cane meant absolutely nothing. They were abused at home. They were used to taking beatings from their drunken fathers. This punishment simply would not work with them. They often stared at me as if to say, "Is that it?"

I rapidly realized that the cane was not the answer. I developed a new approach, and of course this was not popular with the weak teachers, who expected me to exact their revenge. I stopped using the cane. When some of the teachers found out I no longer administered corporal punishment they were not happy. I told them to do their own caning. It was their right to do so, but of course they declined and criticized me for not doing my job. I told them I was doing my job. I had found a better way.

I asked the teachers who referred their students to me to give them schoolwork to bring along. I would supervise them. I left each child in my office on his own to do his assignment and I sat outside. I called this *'solitary one'*. At times during a solitary one the student opened the door, only to be instructed to go back inside and continue working. For the most part the threat of isolation worked, and the teachers who still wanted me to cane their boys slowly came around.

Then there was *'solitary two'*. I applied this when solitary one failed to work, and the boy continued being disruptive when let back into the classroom. What was the difference between solitary one and solitary two?

With solitary one, the boy was deprived of any contact for the whole lesson, but rejoined the class at recess, and then continued the day back in my office. With solitary two, for a hard-core offender, I refused to release him for recess. He could hear all the noise and commotion of recess but could not join his friends. When recess ended, I took the boy out to the playground and let him experience his own solitary recess. Sometimes this was too much to take. Occasionally a boy stopped coming to school.

The headmaster endorsed the policy of troublesome boys not attending school as the answer, even if it contradicted the district wide policy of maintaining attendance standards. His attitude was 'the fewer troublemakers, the better.' The headmaster, Mr. Blacas, left it to the courts to prosecute the parents for non-compliance.

Crime being wrong did not seem to register in this area. I remember dealing with a boy who stole a bicycle. He could not grasp it was wrong. His argument was that it was going to be stolen anyway because it was unlocked.

Disciplining girls was much more difficult. They did not present any physical threats to their teachers. I sympathized with them because most of their problems stemmed from awful situations at home. I heard many horror stories. Some nauseated me. I heard a father was using his twin daughters as prostitutes. There was another story which really tugged at my heartstrings.

I had developed a relationship with John the social worker, who kept me informed of local situations that affected the children at school. He told me the story of Pam, and I knew who he was talking about. She was a quiet unassuming girl who did not attract attention in the classroom. Pam lived alone with her mother. Her father was not around, and her mother was an alcoholic. Pam came home one day to find her mother had hanged herself. Pam was left alone, and social services sent her to a home for juveniles. A year later a social worker who worked at the home was very upset and contacted me. Pam was required to move out of the home because she was too old.

The lady told me Pam worked wonders with the younger girls and acted like another member of the staff. Was there anything I could do?

I never believed in the efficacy of bureaucracy, and I defied the system when I could. After all, rules were made to be broken. In this situation I did not care. Pam was doing great work. She helped the other unfortunate children, and she deserved help if I could do it. I visited the social worker and handed her an envelope. She opened it and looked at me. I said, "Here is Pam's birth certificate. You thought she was sixteen years old, but this indicates she is fifteen." The woman stared at the document. Anybody who really wanted to cause a problem could look closely enough to see an alteration might have been made. It was now up to the social worker. She smiled. I did not hear from her again, or any authorities for that matter. The correct thing had been done, and because there were far too many other serious problems to deal with, I am sure we were right to do what we did.

Many people complimented me for the work I did in my new position. Then a senior teacher told me about an open deputy headmaster position at a school out of the immediate area, but under the same education authority. I was tempted, but one thing bothered me about it. The promotion involved less actual teaching, the job I really enjoyed.

It was time for a change, but more of that later.

STUDENT TRIPS ABROAD.

During my time in Salford, and again after I arrived in the United States, I chaperoned older students on school sponsored European trips. The first of these, when I taught in Salford, was part of the *'twin'* towns and cities program. Below is the definition of the idea.

Town twinning, as an official relationship-builder, started in Europe after the second world war. The idea was simple: repair damaged relationships between France, Germany and the UK. Find towns that suffered during the wars and pair them. Then encourage people from these areas to meet, mix and get along. That's why town twinning – at its core – is a good and important thing.

Salford was twinned with Clermont Ferrand in France, and Lunen in Germany. A city council member had approached Dennis Lester, the head of Broughton High's Art department and married to Judy, the head of the French department, about taking a party of schoolchildren to Clermont Ferrand. Dennis asked me if I would like to go.

I agreed in part because it was a free trip, but also because I was good friends with Dennis, and I had been good at French in high school.

Clermont Ferrand is nothing like Salford, which begs the question 'Why these two towns?' It was a three-way exchange, with Clermont hosting a similar group from their German twin town.

It was a three-week venture, and I enjoyed interacting with teachers and working to improve my French. Even though he married a teacher of French, Dennis did not know the language. The French staff and students liked me, and I am sure it was because I tried to speak their language when possible. We also had an intern whose name escapes me. I think he studied at Salford University.

Near the end of the third week we decided to hold a concert for the students to put on a show. About half-way through, our intern and two of the oldest girls went on stage. They performed a kind of dialogue where they made fun of two of the older French boys in the audience, Serge and Pascal.

Clermont Ferrand, very different from Salford.

British humor is unique. Other countries do not interpret our sarcasm as humorous and can initially take offense. The act clearly did not amuse the French. Serge and Pascal were high profile older members of the French group and they were inseparable. They were extremely embarrassed, and the audience stopped laughing as the act went on. Everyone but the performers thought the act was inappropriate. We could see the French boys talking among themselves and the atmosphere turned nasty.

Dennis ordered the entire staff to take duty that night in the dorms. We sensed trouble. Normally one teacher chaperoned, while the others relaxed over a beer in the staff room. It was a tough night and I did not sleep well, fearing the worst when I woke up. When I did, the intern and the two girls were gone. Dennis had contacted Brian Senior, his superior in Salford, who gave him permission to send the three culprits home immediately by any means possible. It avoided a nasty situation.

I think the French staff appreciated the gesture and in my honest opinion I think they were shocked we went so far, as they had a very laid-back approach to discipline.

The strangest part of the whole cultural exchange was the interaction between the three groups. The visit was designed as a pair of exchanges, French/English and French/German, hosted in France. However, the English and Germans interacted the most. It created a problem when these two groups naturally gravitated to each other. The French constantly reminding us, as I am sure they did with the Germans, it was not an English/German exchange.

The next year we arranged an exchange in Lunen, Salford's German twin town. This time it was a German/English, and a German/French exchange. Judy and Dennis did not want to go, so Brian asked me to lead. I agreed and Jane Ayres, a young French teacher from Broughton High, was my assistant.

It was a different experience. The French leader was a jovial extrovert.

I also fell sick which did not help, but things went smoothly. It still amazes me that during two trips the English and the Germans interacted so well, but it was always hard work with the French.

After I moved to the United States Michael Latcham, a college friend, contacted me and asked me if I wanted to join his school trip. He was taking boys and girls skiing, and he told me if I could get to London, I could join them on a trip to an Italian ski resort. I agreed to meet him at London Airport.

We were on the slopes when, as we were about to descend the last hill to the hotel, Michael called up to me to keep my group at the top of the hill. One of his group had fallen in the middle of the hill, and he was worried about one of my lesser skilled skiers running into his fallen skier on the way down.

I kept my group at the top and it was a long wait. In the bar later Michael said to me, "That is why I brought you. Some of my other teachers in school might not have been able to keep the group at the top of the hill, due to their lack of control and discipline." I took it as a compliment.

Another reason prompted him next year to extend an invitation for me to accompany him on a skiing trip to Bulgaria. I met him as usual at London Airport, and off we went behind the 'Iron Curtain.' It is an experience

I will never forget. Michael, who had previously visited Bulgaria, told me on the airplane why he was giving me another free trip.

"Of course, there is the discipline," he said "but I have another reason. I want you to take charge of all the spending money, because we cannot trust the schoolchildren. They will be approached by people from the black market." Then he looked at me. "We will all be approached by the black marketeers."

I understood immediately what he was suggesting. Something an outsider could get away with. He smiled and went back to his seat.

I did not have to wait long. All tourists were obvious targets, but I had far more money so I could negotiate. I had no trouble getting much more than the exchange rate offered by the bank, and I made sure the children received a better rate. We were careful not to let them know our scheme.

The staff basically wined and dined for free all week, but something changed when we went into the bar for our last night. The prices. Our hosts realized we were no longer of any value to the community. We were leaving, so they extorted us.

Drink prices skyrocketed. It left a nasty taste in our mouths, and I do not mean the drinks. One shady character asked me if I liked the waitresses. I told him they were great, meaning they served us well all week. He looked at me and said, "You want a waitress ...?" I was appalled and just walked away.

Life behind the Iron Curtain......

PART THREE,
THE UNITED STATES.

NOW FOR SOMETHING COMPLETELY DIFFERENT.

In the early 1980s one of my college friends Geoff Illingworth moved to the United States and contacted a few of us about an opportunity in southern California. He was a very funny man and had previously worked for a short time as a teacher, before starting a career as a comedian in the many night clubs of northern England. A few of my friends and I had seen his act.

He was taking a holiday in southern California when he met Hank Berthiaume, who ran a soccer club for boys aged between eight and seventeen. Hank invited Geoff to coach at the club. Geoff figured he could make a living working as a soccer coach for Hank during the school year, especially if he could run summer day camps which could be very lucrative. He invited me to spend my summer holiday working at his soccer camps.

I enjoyed the experience, and shortly after I returned to England, his boss Hank invited me to work full time for the club. The idea of living in southern California and becoming a soccer coach full time appealed to me.

I was a teacher, thirty-three years old, and I wasn't teaching as much as I wanted to due to my promotion. I also had a live-in girlfriend and we were not getting along.

Hank promised enough work for me. I could make money in summer soccer camps. I was ready for a change. I handed in my notice, left a very good teaching job with excellent prospects, and flew to California to work as a full-time assistant coach to my college friend Geoff.

I should have done more research and asked for some guarantees. After I started working with Geoff, he made it clear to Hank if there was more work available, and consequently more money, he was the one who should earn it. This meant less for me.

I realized then what Geoff wanted from me was an English companion who understood his humor. He led me on with promises of more work in the summer at camps. The coaching job was in fact not full time. It was very much part time and I was running out of money.

I had stayed in touch with my friends in Salford and was surprised to hear there was a chance for me to go home, and work as an assistant to my friend Walt. It was a contract for one year. I accepted the offer, but I knew that with proper planning I could return to the States and carve out a successful life in southern California.

Hank stayed in touch, encouraged me to return, and promised full time work. Geoff also encouraged me and made the same promise. There was a slight hitch, however. I had returned to my former school in England and accepted a contract for one year. If I completed it, I received summer vacation pay. Geoff and Hank needed me back for the summer. Geoff had camp commitments, and he wanted me to work with him, but I decided to stay in England and collect the summer vacation money. I think they both felt I let them down, but I did return to the States, just later in the summer than they wanted. I did work their camps for what I thought was minimal money. I was right to stay in England and collect the six weeks of vacation money.

Geoff arranged for me to live with a mutual friend, Mike Martucci, to whom I paid rent. He had the bedroom and I slept on a pull-out couch in the other room. Mike was a neatness freak. He constantly complained about small blades of grass that came off my shoes and clothing. I needed a place of my own, but I got a shock when the summer ended. I earned $600.00 a month in the summer but I took a pay cut to coach in the fall. This was because many of our boys were playing for their high school, so there were less boys for us to coach. My wages were reduced to $400.00 a month, barely enough to cover my rent. This was not what I envisaged. I was not happy with Hank.

I was forced to find another job. I worked as a bus boy, until the restaurant owner discovered he could not pay me. My visa had been granted to me as a soccer coach, a vocation where my expertise was considered something the country at the time was short of. I had brought some money with me, but I was anxious not to depend on it. I wanted to start a life in the States where I could make a living for myself.

I had left a complex relationship in England. Pauline White, the woman I had been dating for over a year, moved in with me just before I began my American adventure. Though the relationship was over, I continued to pay the monthly mortgage, electricity, water and rates bills. In the year before returning to the States I moved back to the house. She was not happy, and it was a difficult but manageable situation that was going to change.

Once I returned to the States for good, I contacted her about the house. I wanted the matter resolved and asked her to pay me my half of the equity. It was a very good deal for her. She was literally gaining a half share of equity in the house, something she had paid absolutely nothing into. When I lived with her, she was only responsible for our food. I paid every other bill.

Her mother intervened. She claimed I left her daughter, so the house belonged to Pauline. I informed her that she did not have a court case. She would probably lose, and even if she did win, it would not be worth her effort once she paid the legal bills. It took me forever to convince her that the longer she delayed, the more my half share increased. This was because house prices were soaring. Pauline eventually, to the disdain of her mother, gave in.

The money from the house settlement served as my security blanket. It was not much, but I could pursue my goal to become solvent in the States. However, another piece of good fortune soon made it easier. A part time soccer coaching job at one of the local universities became available. The University of California at San Diego needed a women's soccer coach.

INTRODUCTION TO COLLEGE COACHING.

Hank and Geoff didn't mind me working for a college, even though the practice times and travel meant they had to rearrange the whole schedule. They understood I needed more money and were happy it was coming from a source outside the club. I had no idea what to expect after I was hired by UCSD. I did not completely understand the restrictions placed on college coaches regarding practice and competition seasons, but I knew I still had a short time to coach the team in the spring of 1984.

I met the team for a coaching session. I was shocked when only seven women showed up. There had obviously been previous problems. Either players quit, or maybe they did not want the commitment. Whatever the reason I did not have a lot of time before the competition season started. I still needed to complete the schedule of games to be played for the next season.

I also needed players. I ran a good coaching session that day and I asked if they knew other players. Nine attended the next session and the word spread. I also found a list of recruits who may have written or had contact. I worked the phones to try to find more players.

We began the August pre-season with thirteen players and the possibility that more would join us when classes started. That did not happen overnight, and we had games to play. UCSD was the only Division III women's team in California at the time.

My mother and father visited me in San Diego.

I inherited a schedule comprised of Division I, II, and independent club teams. We were heading into a very daunting season.

My players could not have been a finer bunch of young women. They totally believed in me, and even though we were outclassed by superior opposition, we managed to compete. I can remember losing 0-2 to UC Santa Barbara, a Division I university, and they had Carin Jennings a future national team player on their team. We added a few players as the season went on, but I was determined to recruit for the following season. I also wanted to find an easier schedule which was problematic because Division III women's soccer was still in its infancy in California.

In my three years at UCSD the record of the team improved dramatically. In 1984, my first year, the record was 3-12-3. In 1985 we improved to 9-10-2 and in 1986 the team went 15-5-4.

UCSD Women's team during my second year.

I was enjoying life as a college coach, but it was a part time job. In order to make it full time I needed to teach five classes in the physical education department. After I taught my first soccer class it was very popular, so the administration gave me three classes the following year, because so many students had signed up. I felt confident I could get to five. I could teach far more than just soccer.

THE MINNESOTA CONNECTION.

I always had to decide what to do during the summer when college was out. Mostly I would do camps with Geoff in other areas. Soccer camps meant good money. Hank offered a team package opportunity to groups who entered his 'Mission Bay Classic' summer tournament. It included the chance for players and teams to be coached by a professional coach. A team from Minnesota took this offer and I coached them for the days leading up to the tournament.

This connection proved very fruitful. There were many San Diego area coaches who sponsored summer soccer camps, so there was little room for me. I needed to decide how to supplement my income in the summer, and the club from Minnesota suggested I could earn good money by running summer camps there. I could coach the Northwest Soccer Club, one of the largest clubs in Minnesota.

The San Diego teams took the summer off and I could earn much more working in Minnesota than in San Diego. I also did not have to pay rent. I could live in the home of a local coach Al Schaaf, who planned to spend his summer in Germany. It was more work, but it was also more money. I decided to go to Minnesota for three months to coach the Northwest Soccer Club. It was a soccer club for boys only.

Northwest was formed by merging the players from two northwest suburban high schools, Cooper and Armstrong, to form a very large soccer club. The first thing they wanted me to do was select three teams by ability, during two days of try outs they had set up.

I was horrified on the first day when I saw how they conducted try outs. Their committee set up stations for drills. I learned later this was standard practice for ice hockey and of course Minnesota is the 'State of Hockey'. The committee members staffed each station and graded the players on their ability to dribble round cones, and other pertinent skills.

We met later that night to discuss the next day's drills, and how I planned to use the scores to select the teams. They received a shock. I told them I would completely take over the next day. I told them soccer player's abilities need to be judged by their game speed decisions, plus other concepts you could not measure with drills. I told them I planned to organize the players into eleven versus eleven games, and then I would select three eighteen member teams. They were shocked, but I told them I was the soccer coach they hired for the summer. I took full responsibility even if my selection did not work out. I was going to put the players in the right positions for three different teams, based on their ability in game situations.

They agreed, so I set up the games and let the players choose their positions. Each game lasted about twenty minutes. I took notes and changed the player's positions as I saw fit. I also started rearranging the players until I produced three eighteen player teams. I used the full two hours and I told the committee I would meet them later in the evening to give my final selections.

We met at a house in Plymouth and I shared my first second and third team choices. I reminded them I was the only person in the room who did not have a son playing in the club. I had no conflict of interest. I pointed out that since I was making the team selections, they could not accuse me of playing favorites. I told them to refer complaining parents to me if they did not like the selections.

When I announced the teams one member immediately announced his displeasure. He confronted me and asked how I could possibly place Phil in the second team and John in the first? He said Phil was the best hockey player in the state and a superb athlete, whereas John was much smaller. I asked him what on earth hockey had to do with choosing a soccer team? I told him Phil was clearly uncomfortable with the ball and I failed to understand for one moment how hockey played a part in anything. I said, "One of the reasons you hired me is because very few people at this table know anything about soccer. Now you are telling me, somebody who has played and coached this game all his life, that you might now think you know more than me."

Another committee member apologized, but there was more. Tom, who brought the matter up, said there was no way he could call Phil that night and tell him he was on the second team. I looked round the table. "This is why you hired me. Parents are not going to question me about my decisions and even if they do, I have no personal stake in the club other than being hired to produce the best teams. I will call every family and tell them which team I have selected for their son."

It is ironic that the under sixteen team, the group involved in the Phil and John controversy, later won the State Cup producing one of the biggest upsets in Minnesota State Cup history. The team defeated two perennial powerhouses who had always contested the final, the Blackhawks of St Paul and the Rochester Arrows. They beat one team in the semifinal and the other in the final. I heard this in California, as I had returned to take up my college coaching position just before the Minnesota state tournament finals.

An interesting thing happened later that year. I was in a San Diego supermarket when a man stopped me to congratulate me on our state championship in Minnesota. He explained his son played on the Rochester Arrows, the team we beat in the semifinal. He had heard about me. Stories about the upsets had spread, and people understood it was because Northwest had hired a certain professional coach.

It turns out he was Charlie, the father of Mark Abboud, who later played for me at Macalester College. Mark really wanted to play Division I soccer, but his father was far more interested in his son's education and sent him to Macalester. He told him he would play for a very good coach. I spoke with Mark long after he graduated and reminded him of the story. He said "Yes, it was the best decision I never made."

DIVISION III HAS A NEW CHAMPIONSHIP.

In 1985 the NCAA announced the creation of a Division III National Championship for women's soccer, to be held in the fall of 1986. The sport was growing, colleges were adding soccer to their athletic budgets. We managed to stay around .500 for the 1985 season but still did not have a Division III opponent on our schedule. 1986 changed for the better. I had recruited a large class of first year players, and they comprised exactly half our roster.

The NCAA divided the country into eight regions, and because there were so few Division III teams in California, the newly created West Region stretched from the west coast all the way to Minnesota. The Minnesota Intercollegiate Athletic Conference is a strong Division III conference. The regional committee needed a California representative to inform the national committee about tournament quality teams from our region. At that time, I coached the only Division III women's team in California. Like it or not, I had to serve.

In my third year the young players I recruited helped us to an outstanding season. We won fifteen games and created a problem in our NCAA region. Our region was so big California teams did not play mid-west opponents. How could we determine which teams should represent our region in national competition when we had not seen each other play? I felt confident my fellow committee members would recognize our successful season, where we hardly played any Division III teams, yet had fifteen wins. They did not. I felt uncomfortable about pushing my team, but it soon became clear the other committee members thought the mid-west teams were better. They did not know California soccer. The weekly rankings always listed UCSD as third or fourth in the region.

I had to say something. I was not speaking out of turn because I knew California soccer, and I knew Minnesota soccer from working there in the summer. My committee members also told me how tough it was going to be for the West Region, because the east coast committee members believed they played a better brand of soccer there.

In the last committee phone call, we were about to rank UCSD third behind two colleges from Minnesota, when I spoke about my knowledge of both states. I assured them the California soccer standard was much higher, as I had personal experience of coaching youth soccer in both states at the highest level. I said this was an informed opinion, I had traveled back and forth for a couple of years.

One of our more experienced committee members commented that the east coast members would make sure the west received only two spots in the playoffs, far fewer than the two east coast regions. They wanted to include three teams from each of the east coast regions and reduce the number of west region teams. I managed to convince fellow committee members that by ranking UCSD as our region's number one team, which was the right thing to do, it would also very likely ensure the inclusion of three west region teams in the tournament. This was because one of the two teams from Minnesota we were including in our rankings, St. Mary's, had beaten some east coast teams and showed they deserved selection.

The west region committee accepted my reasoning but unfortunately, the national committee selected only one Minnesota team. They still believed the east coast teams played the best brand of women's soccer. They selected UCSD plus St. Mary's from Minnesota. They added Methodist College from North Carolina as the third west region representative. The good news however was two teams needed to fly to the regionals. It was early November so it made sense to pick the venue where weather would not ruin the tournament. As the number one seed UCSD would play the winner of a game between the other two.

It was of course a huge advantage for us to watch two teams play a game the day before the winner played us. It was a chance to scout them, plus we rested on a day when our opponent was playing. We would have fresher legs.

During half time of the play-in game I needed to have a word with my team. They were laughing joking and very excited, and I knew why. We were watching teams that did not play up to our standard. Both teams were much slower, less athletic, and my team knew it. I warned them about betraying their emotions and made it clear they must take the next day's game seriously.

We received an additional advantage when the scoreless game went to overtime resulting in a penalty shootout, which St. Mary's won. I thought we should be very confident when we took the field for the championship match. St. Mary's had played an overtime game the day before. We knew we were more athletic than them in every position. What I did not know was whether playing our first ever playoff game would make us nervous. St. Mary's had already experienced and coped with that feeling.

We dominated the play in the championship match, but we simply failed to press home our superiority and we could not score. The game went into overtime and remained scoreless. Then it dawned on me: penalty kicks would decide the outcome.

The fear of being the superior team and losing on penalty kicks is so real. Penalty kick results are not determined by better players or athletes or anything else. Penalty kick shootouts really come down to players managing their nerves under pressure. If anything, St. Mary's had to feel better than we did. They had been involved in a shootout the day before. For the first time in the game they must have felt they had a chance of winning.

A coach is a fool if he does not have his team practice penalty shootouts for the playoffs. I had selected my five in my head the day before, when we practiced taking kicks. I made sure each player took only one practice shot against our starting keeper. It did not make sense to have them take another because our keeper would know their intentions. After taking another try against our back up keeper, I had them practice shooting into an empty net. I wanted them to have the confidence of seeing the ball hit the net. I also told our keepers if they were involved in a shootout they must not guess. There is a strong chance of a player mishitting the ball and for the keeper to dive the wrong way when an easy save was possible.

I told my two best penalty takers to go first. There is no point in keeping them back, as it might result in them not kicking. But what about the fifth penalty try which could be the decider? Here is where I was lucky. We had Toni Krumme, a defender with quite simply the most powerful kick I have ever seen on a women's soccer player. I said "Toni, just hit it as hard as you can and keep it under the crossbar."

We scored two, then missed one. They scored two, then missed two. We scored, they scored. It came down to Toni and her power. She blasted the ball just past the left ear of their keeper, who could not move. We had won, and we were going to New York for the Final Four.

THE FINAL FOUR.

In the modern era the NCAA predetermines the Final Four is played at a neutral location, and it is always staged in a place where hopefully the weather will not be a factor. Throughout the 1986 playoffs the first Division III women's championship national committee remained conscious of transportation costs in assigning sites. This was a determining factor in the opening rounds. With the fewer west coast colleges, the committee had no choice.

The team of the Final Four. Back row far left, Erin Aafedt and Stacy Simmon, who had graduated and stayed as assistants.

There were three east coast colleges in the Final Four. There was no doubt we would be flying east.

We flew out on Thursday to Syracuse, New York to play in the Final Four at Cortland State University. The team was very excited. When we practiced the next day on Cortland State's game field, we were surprised to find a thin layer of snow covering the field. Almost our entire team grew up in California. The only time they had seen snow was when they went skiing, they had never played soccer on snow.

They had fun at practice, but I was concerned. The other teams had played in these conditions at the end of their seasons, probably on several occasions, whether playing for their high school or college. Even worse the weather warmed on the morning of our semifinal with the University of Rochester. The snow had melted, but the ground underneath was still partly frozen. Players really had problems keeping their feet. Playing good soccer in these conditions was impossible. The team from nearby Rochester, New York clearly had an

86

advantage, although I must say that Rochester draws students from around the country. However, their coach was from the northeast and so were most of his players.

Rochester dominated us from the opening kickoff, as we struggled with the conditions. They scored two early goals and we were lucky to only be down only 0-2 at half time. As the field turned to mud it became a little easier, but the California players had not played much in mud either. We held on but did not threaten Rochester. We finally lost the game 0-2. I could see the disappointment on my player's faces.

They did not understand why we played in such atrocious conditions, and why we played in a place where the championship organizers knew that weather conditions could ruin a game. I understood their attitude but knew they were naïve.

Finances meant everything to the new Division III championship committee. It was much cheaper to stage the games in New York than it was to fly three teams to California. The issue of travel financing would continue to influence site decisions for many years. Ultimately that policy did change but I knew my players, and the players immediately following them, would never host an NCAA Division III championship. We would always have to fly to the east coast.

I watched the other semifinal between Cortland State and Plymouth State, which the latter won 3-2. There was an incident later at the bar with the Cortland coach Chris Malone. It likely stemmed from something I said the night before at the banquet. The coaches were seated with the NCAA officials, and Chris complained there was no seat for his wife. He kept on and on, saying "Where is my wife going to sit? What am I going to tell my wife?" I politely said "Chris, just tell her she can sit with all the other wives at the wives table next to ours." He just glared at me.

After our semifinal loss I was standing at the bar with Terry Gurnett, the Rochester coach. Suddenly Chris interrupted and said to me "I knew a California team should not have been selected, your team did not try hard out there." I was angry and immediately went back at him "My players played their hardest, and even though the conditions were tough for us, how dare you accuse them of not trying? At least we did not lose the way your team did. Your team lost because you gave up three goals playing that stupid offside trap. You, the coach, can take the blame for that. You should go apologize to your team." Chris stormed off.

Terry looked at me and said "Let me buy you a drink. You just did what so many coaches up here have wanted to do for years. You put him in his place."

Terry and I have stayed friends for years. Later when he chaired the Division III All America committee, I called him with a problem. I was a regional chair and I told him I was going to fire one of my committee members. I said he consistently promoted his own players. Terry told me not to fire him. I was shocked. He then said it was 'his job' as national chair, and he would gladly take care of it, which he subsequently did. Although we have not talked all that much since, we have stayed good friends and we made sure to congratulate each other on our subsequent retirements.

The team flight back was a great deal of fun. We had lost, but we sensed we would be back. Half our travel squad were first year players. We learned that we could compete at the highest level in Division III and we were much more experienced than the new programs emerging in California.

A FULL TIME COLLEGE SOCCER COACH.

My 1986 UCSD experience convinced me that I wanted to be a full-time college soccer coach. All I needed was to increase my teaching load to five classes. Importantly I had never had a job in California that offered benefits, most essential of which was health care. It looked to me with the popularity of my soccer class that it was just a matter of time.

Hank and Geoff were good about allowing me to coach at UCSD, even though it complicated their schedule. I think Geoff was pleased I did not take any work away from him. Money motivated Geoff. He earned a great deal of money from his night club comedy act in England, but his act was not suited to American audiences. He was not getting enough work and he had come to the States determined to succeed. You could make money by working summer camps if you were prepared to travel. Geoff was ambitious. He ventured into outlying areas like Bakersfield to work camps. I worked for him as often as I could, but my heart was now elsewhere.

Hank paid Geoff and me from the large profit he made from his Mission Bay Classic tournament. However, he made the mistake of not pursuing his own computer diagnostic business enough, relying on club funds, which now meant three full time personnel. There were also some people working to undermine his tournament.

To make matters worse, our coaching situation was getting complicated. Geoff and Hank started arguing. Hank tried to repair their relationship by offering Geoff bonuses if the teams won. It was a huge mistake. Geoff became very irritated when his young boys made mistakes, and his behavior on the sidelines left something to be desired. Hank often came off the field during a game to complain to me about how agitated Geoff was becoming. I told Hank it was his fault for paying win bonuses, but Hank was frustrated. He told me he was planning to fire Geoff, and he asked me to take Geoff's place. I told Hank I was not interested but it put me in a bind. How long could I work for Hank when I refused to take what he was offering me? Though I wanted to be a full-time college coach, I still needed to work for the Mission Bay Soccer Club to supplement my UCSD income.

In the meantime, Geoff was complaining to me about his relationship with Hank. He suggested that we both work for another club. I was not interested in that either. I wanted to be a full-time college coach and was working hard to make that happen, but I needed the Mission Bay work. I told Geoff I was prepared to go to the edge of the cliff with him, but I would not jump off.

Hank fired Geoff and Geoff immediately told the boy's parents that I was in on it. He said I wanted his job. It was untrue, and I suffered plenty of abuse, but I needed the job. What I really wanted was to teach two more classes at UCSD and leave Mission Bay behind.

Geoff was one of the best soccer coaches I knew when it came to teaching boys in coaching sessions lasting two hours. I learned a great deal from him. We both had coaching licenses from coaching schools in England. I was one of the few who qualified first time.

To replace Geoff, Hank hired Gerd Wiejerkowski a former professional player, who had recently retired from the local pro team, the San Diego Sockers. Gerd had no coaching license and just let the players play. He told Hank it was embarrassing for a former professional player with a local reputation to be an assistant to me. Hank asked me if it was alright for us both to be head coaches. I agreed even though I knew Gerd was undermining me to Hank. However, it was Hank who came to me to complain about Gerd just letting the boys play.

BOMBSHELL.

I felt confident I would soon obtain the requisite five classes I needed to work full time at UCSD. Doug Dannevik, the volleyball coach, had recently done the same thing so he had cleared a path for me. Besides, soccer was more popular than volleyball. Our athletic director, Judy Sweet, had just reviewed my player evaluations with me. She said they were the best she had ever seen, so I knew I had a good chance. Once my position was full time with benefits, I planned to drop the Mission Bay work and supplement my income by running camps at UCSD.

Then the bombshell fell. UCSD dropped their physical education program, an announcement that shocked me and devastated Doug. He had just become full time. He had health insurance. Now he had nothing. He needed to find a new job. He told me he had lived in California his entire life and did not want to leave the state. He did not know what to do and neither did I.

I did not feel much better than Doug. Though I never really had the full time UCSD job he had, I had come so close. I really wanted to be a college coach full time. I decided to apply for jobs all over the country.

WHERE DO I GO?

One of the curious aspects of college coaching is the predictable nature of the way administrators hire coaches. They follow a familiar pattern. I knew I would be immediately ruled out of the running for any Division I or Division II positions, because athletic directors tend to hire assistants from within the division. Upper level administrators look down on Division III coaches. They view them as being less competitive. I knew I could coach up a level. By 1986 my record against Division II teams was 8-0. It might have been even better, but several Division II teams stopped scheduling my Division III UCSD team after we beat them.

I applied here, there, and anywhere for a women's, or men's head coaching position when they became available, mostly to no avail. Then I got a break. St. Mary's University in Minnesota wanted to interview me for the men's head coaching position. I imagine Dan Blank, the St. Mary's women's coach I had met in the regional playoffs, had seen my application and had recommended me to his boss.

At this point the story of how I got my Macalester coaching position becomes very complicated, especially because two of the people involved in it, Jim Beaton and Ed Cochrane, have passed away. They cannot verify the facts. Consequently, I am drawing on my own memory of the process. Jim is at the center of the story, but it is also necessary to understand Ed wanted to become a business associate in my future camp endeavors. What follows is ninety per cent fact and ten per cent personal assumption. Here is what I believe happened.

From the time after I coached the Northwest Soccer Club at the Mission Bay Classic, and then spent my summers coaching in Minnesota, I was asked what it would take for me to move to Minnesota and coach the club and camps there. I always insisted I would move for a college position if it was full time, and since I thought I was going to be full time at UCSD, I generally brushed the idea off.

I kept in constant contact with Ed, who was very keen to help me make money with a large soccer camp enterprise in Minnesota during the summer. We spent long hours on the phone and created a company called 'Soccerworld.' Ed was so enthusiastic he even put up the money. When I called them to say I was going to be interviewed at St. Mary's both he and Jim were excited.

Jim worked at the University of Minnesota in human resources. He came up with a rather strange idea. He told me he wanted to make the most of my trip to Minnesota. He asked me to interview at Macalester College, for the purpose of getting my interview on file.

I remember when I interviewed at Macalester, the Athletic Director Sheila Brewer asked me why we were conducting this interview. I told her that my friend Jim, who worked in human resources at the University of

Minnesota, had recommended it. He thought it might help because he knew there were many small colleges in Minnesota. The more I put my name in the running for jobs, the better chance I had of getting an interview and landing a head coaching position.

I think Jim also had an ulterior motive. His daughter played for Macalester. The players on the Macalester men's team had told her their coach was awful. They said he knew absolutely nothing about soccer. They were upset especially because they believed they had a good team. Jim also had a son Andy who was a very good high school player and Jim wanted him to go to Macalester. He also wanted him to have a good coach.

In the 1980s most full time Division III coaches coached two sports. This factor led me eventually to turn down the St. Mary's offer because it involved coaching women's softball, a sport I knew nothing about. I could not fathom how a coach could accept the job on those terms. Macalester also had a dual coaching philosophy. In their case the men's soccer coach also served as head coach of men's track and field.

During my Macalester interview Sheila made it absolutely clear she did not know why she was interviewing me, and she was puzzled by my explanation of getting an interview on file. She also had an obligation to Greg Hunter, her current head soccer coach. She went to great lengths to tell him she did not agree with the interview.

When Greg found out about my interview, he tried to contact me immediately. He wanted me to know there was a possible opening for me. He explained he and his wife were unhappy in Minnesota. They wanted to return to the east coast. He told me that two Macalester professors, a husband and wife, had shared one position. He asked me, if it could be arranged, to consider sharing his job for one year. I would coach soccer and he would coach track and field. Then he would leave, and the job would be mine.

He approached Sheila with the idea of job sharing. Sheila was a difficult boss. Virtually the entire staff disliked her and avoided her at all costs. She was abrasive, rude and demanding. I think she took pleasure in putting people down. She ruled discussion free staff meetings with an iron fist. I would develop a very stormy relationship with her, and I was not the only one.

She immediately explained our planned job sharing was not as easy as it looked. The two professors who had previously shared a single job were married, so it was easy for them to share benefits. She told me I would earn half Greg's salary but would not be eligible for benefits. She said Greg had a wife. He needed to keep the benefits. I did not argue. I could wait one more year to fulfill my ambition to be a full-time college coach.

I moved to Minnesota just before the fall season. I had been in touch with the captains and was pleased by their positive reception. The whole team showed up to help me move into my apartment. They really wanted to tell me how bad a coach Greg was, but out of professional courtesy I refused to listen. Sheila quickly made it clear to me that Greg had recruited a great class the previous year, but that was to become a matter of opinion.

A TEAM HAPPY TO SEE ME.

I only needed one coaching session to know the whole team was delighted with the coaching change. After a very poor season the previous year and playing for a coach who had no idea about soccer, they were very pleased to play for one who apparently knew what he was doing.

Though Sheila always found a way to be negative, she told me she expected the team to improve. The 'outstanding class' Greg had recruited the year before were now sophomores. This is a team that failed to win a conference game the previous year. Clearly, they were not that good. Fortunately, a couple of players who quit the year before rejoined the team, but we started the pre-season before Macalester's new international students arrived. A few players, namely Wayne Markman from South Africa, Nicky Larsson from Sweden, and Christos Ioannides from Cyprus did play for us that year, and it started a trend. I was very interested in recruiting some more international players.

We added players to our roster. Some American students now wanted to play because they heard it was going to be a good experience. Some had not been recruited. I welcomed them all. The better teams in the MIAC had junior varsity teams and I wanted Macalester to have one too.

We did not have enough players to run separate varsity and junior varsity teams. If a substitute varsity player did not play anywhere near a full game, I put him on the roster for the next junior varsity game and told the coach to play him for the whole game. I used the JV squad as a reserve team like they do in the professional leagues. The JV games gave players a chance to show if they deserved to move up to the varsity.

The only problem with my plan was that the MIAC only permitted players to compete in eighteen games and they counted both varsity and JV games. I ignored it. How could playing as a substitute for five minutes count as a game?

A famous college basketball coach once admitted in an interview to something he said to his top new recruits, once they were committed to his program. He said, "My job now is to go out and find somebody better than you, and who can take your place." It sounds like a nasty statement, but it is in fact what good college coaches do, and that is exactly what I did.

The players who once welcomed me with open arms when they were sophomores, did not like me very much by the time they were seniors. I had recruited better players. That was my job. I wanted to win. A couple of years after this group of disgruntled seniors graduated, one sent a letter of complaint to Macalester

President Bob Gavin and a few other administrators. He urged the college to fire me. President Gavin did not share this letter with me, but I found out.

My biggest recruiting coup came shortly after I arrived on campus. The previous summer I was coaching camps in California when a fellow coach at the camp from New Zealand asked me if I would be interested in recruiting a couple of players from his country. They were obviously talented. The New Zealand soccer federation was interested in inviting them to play for their younger age national teams. It is an interesting story.

All admissions offices in selective schools such as Macalester set enrollment goals. A college needs to bring a certain number of students to campus each year in order to balance its books, and selective schools are very interested in international students. The more countries represented in an entering class, the better it makes the college look. I knew Macalester liked to brag about international diversity. It did not take long for me to ask the admissions office if we had any students from New Zealand. We did not, so I knew I had a window of opportunity.

I contacted the two players, Matt Jackson and Roger Bridge. Matt was very interested but did not have the academic record that Macalester requires for admission. His friend Roger was a much better student but planned to stay home and enroll at the University of Auckland.

Our international counsellor Jimm Crowder proved to be the very best admissions officer I ever worked with. Unlike his counterparts he liked athletics. He always looked for students who could help our teams. He was interested in Roger because he was certain to be admitted. He also told me Matt was not academically qualified. I knew the admissions office really wanted to enroll a student from New Zealand. My problem was that Matt was the one most interested in coming, Roger was looking forward to going to Auckland University.

I explained my dilemma to Jimm. Roger had a good offer from Auckland University. He had a reason to stay home. Matt was the key. He was very interested in Macalester. If we failed to admit him Roger would not come to the United States on his own. But if we did admit Matt there was a good chance Roger would come along, and they were both very good soccer players.

Jimm understood. He worked his magic. He convinced admissions director Bill Shain to accept them. Matt and Roger joined a recruiting class that included another excellent player, Mark Abboud. He is the American student who once told me that coming to Macalester was the 'best decision I never made.' The trio had an immediate impact on the 1988 season. I put all three into our midfield and they had different

Help from afar

Matthew Jackson (8) and Roger Bridge of New Zealand are part of Macalester's foreign conne...

Matt and Roger drew newspaper coverage.

skills. Roger was more defensive minded, while Mark played out wide. Matt was a powerful player. He simply drove through midfield.

We really attracted attention when we pulled off a major MIAC upset over St. John's, beating them soundly 3-0. This, even though we lost our starting keeper Mike Cohen to a broken leg, halfway through the season.

We flew to San Diego for the playoffs and were beaten 6-1 by a superior UCSD team, who went on to be national champions. It was like men versus boys, but we found out how good we needed to be.

MEANWHILE BACK AT THE RANCH.

Sheila called me into the office not long after I returned from San Diego. I thought it was to congratulate me and the team on a fine season, but she had other ideas. She was reorganizing Greg's position in the wake of his departure. The position, head coach of men's soccer and men's track and field, the job Greg offered me, was no longer an option. She was hiring a coach for men's cross country and men's track and field. She was turning the men's soccer coaching position into a part time job.

I reminded her of our team's achievement in an athletic department starved for success. I told her she had betrayed me. She denied she ever promised me the job. Greg promised it to me, she did not. I looked at her and said, "But you were aware of his promise" and I added "You could have informed both Greg and I you would not support my hiring."

Sheila was not fazed, not bothered one bit. I remember much later, after we had a blazing row in her office, an odd thing happened. She called to me as I started leaving and asked me to come back. She wore a strange smile as she said, "Thank you." I formed the distinct impression that she enjoyed our confrontations.

I told Sheila what to do with her part time offer. I left and headed home. I ran into Bill Shain, the Director of Admissions, walking across campus. Bill really liked me. I had recruited international students from countries previously not represented in Mac's student body. Our success also helped recruit full pay students from east coast private schools, where soccer was big. I made his office look good. He asked, "How is it going?"

I was still angry and replied, "I can tell you this. I am leaving." He immediately stopped and asked what was wrong. I told him and said I would be leaving Macalester.

Bill frowned and looked at me, "Please do not do anything today, I have a meeting with the president later and I know he will not be happy."

I worked for three presidents at Macalester and Bob Gavin was by far the best. He was a former athlete, and I found out later he had invited Matt and Roger to dinner once he heard about them. The college was well known for holding internationalism as one of its core values. I can only assume that later in the day Bill reported what he heard from me directly to the president.

Sheila called me into her office the following day. She did not mince words. She informed me she had been ordered to create a position for me. She was hiring me as head coach of men's soccer and men's track and field. I could see that she was not happy about being told what to do or how to run her department. Our relationship would deteriorate and become an icy one from that time forward.

Once I got the position, I began looking at the track team to see what I needed to do for the season. I had learned about track from my time with Roy at Salford Grammar Tech and I put my knowledge to work.

I considered the 4x100m relay to be one of my specialties, where the common practice was to assign the anchor leg to the fastest runner. I placed our two fastest runners in the second and third positions, the places where runners covered the most distance. It made complete sense to me and the runners agreed. I helped the triple jumpers improve their marks by making them cover equal distances in each of the three phases. I worked with the hurdlers making sure they kept rhythm in their strides between the hurdles.

My track coaching experience had been at the high school level. I now coached athletes who had worked with high school coaches. This was a minor setback, but it really did not matter.

I was involved in overseeing the whole track and field program, the main part of which was finding assistant coaches for the individual events. I spent most of my time hiring assistants, scheduling our competitions, and most importantly recruiting many different types of track athletes. It was a demanding job where I did little actual coaching.

This was a pre cell phone era. Virtually every coach used a land line in 1987 and there was no e mail. It was customary for Macalester coaches to spend countless evening office hours making recruiting calls. As many as seven or eight coaches would be calling on any given night. Football assistants were frequently in the office but recruiting for the other sports fell into the laps of the head coaches.

Because we spent long hours in the office it didn't take long to make friends with Ken Andrews, the women's soccer coach, and the newly hired women's basketball coach John Hershey, who joined us in October 1986. John also coached softball as his second assignment; Ken supervised the intramural program for his.

Usually around 9.30 pm, John, Ken and I went for a drink nearby. We could not help discussing how to improve the department, how hard it was to work with Sheila, and what the future held for our respective teams. We also expressed our frustration with the football staff. They did not mix with the rest of us and seemed to care only about the football program.

At some point that winter Ken decided he wanted to give up coaching the women's team. There was a department opening and he could run the work study program as his other assignment.

I had an idea. What if I coached both soccer teams? Our stadium had lights so scheduling, the main issue, could be managed. I also had an answer for the people who thought I could not coach separate practices, two hours in duration, for each team. My teams never practiced that long. I usually coached sessions that were an hour long at most. My assistants could warm the players up. I was also in favor of more time off. I wanted my players fresh for games. Of course, I had one major obstacle to overcome: my boss.

I broached the idea with Sheila. I reasoned that the change would help achieve her goal of partnering the men's track and field and men's cross-country programs. John was new on campus. He had no history with Sheila, he could talk to her. He lobbied for the change and finally Sheila agreed. I think she wanted to see me fail.

However, I knew I could do it. There was a precedent. Anson Dorrance coached both teams at the University of North Carolina and was very successful. The only difference between his situation and mine was that he had full time assistant coaches. That did not matter to me. I was determined to make it succeed.

I needed to depend heavily on my part time assistants, and I needed to be very creative with my scheduling. The men played their conference midweek games on Tuesdays or Wednesdays, and the women alternated days with them. The MIAC arranged it this way to accommodate the assignment of officials. It was easy to coach a men's game on Tuesday and a women's game on Wednesday. However, both teams played on Saturdays. That presented a problem.

The other conference coaches were very flexible. I had a good relationship with all of them and I think at first, they genuinely wanted to help. I also think some believed this would weaken our teams. They agreed to schedule some of our home Saturday games on Friday nights.

My plan was working out.

CHANGE.

John Hershey, the women's basketball coach, would go to the office on a Sunday afternoon around 2.00 pm and hit the phones making recruiting calls. He was still there when Ken and I would arrive early evening. We typically stopped calling and adjourned for drinks around 9.30 pm. One Sunday afternoon John arrived to find Sheila cleaning out her office. When he asked her what she was doing, Sheila told him she had been fired.

It had been some time since my campus encounter with Bill Shain, when he told me he would speak to the president on my behalf. I think Sheila's treatment of me triggered some alarm bells among the college big wigs. I think they started paying more attention to the Athletic Department after that. They took notes and built their case against her. Several coaches who left Macalester had cited their inability to get along with the athletic director as one of the reasons they left. It became clear Sheila was never going to provide enough department stability to help coaches produce winning teams, and I had proved winning was possible.

I found out later the decision to fire Sheila was not finalized until there was consultation with our female coaches. The administration needed to know if gender issues were at the heart of the problem. Obviously, the women coaches thought a change advisable.

John called us and reported what he had heard that afternoon. Our evening gathering at the bar was far more enjoyable. That Monday, at our staff meeting, we were told to elect our own leader until a job search could be conducted to fill the position permanently. It was a very interesting meeting.

Football coach Tom Hosier approached me immediately after the meeting. He wanted the job and he thought I could help influence the staff to elect him. This was a mistake. The last thing I wanted was a football coach to lead the department. I liked Tom but since soccer and football used the same field, having a football coach as a boss was a non-starter.

John Hershey also wanted the job. It was a great opportunity, and becoming an athletic director was a career goal for him. Then Ken Andrews threw his hat in the ring. Ken had worked longer than John at Mac and he was an alum. John respected that and immediately withdrew his name. The last thing he wanted was to split the vote, which might result in Tom getting the job. He told me later he also did not want a football coach as athletic director, so as soon as there was an alternative he dropped out.

In his new administrative position as director of intramurals and work study, Ken had demonstrated that he was a capable leader and an efficient administrator. I was not the only one to recognize his good qualities. We voted him in.

From the start Ken showed his talent for taking care of several things at once. The department ran smoothly under his guidance, and what is more we still managed to grab a beer at the end of a night's work.

Tom Hosier accepted the staff's decision. His job was secure. A team he coached ended football's famous fifty game losing streak, a reputation which plagued the department for years and was a national embarrassment. I could get along with Tom very easily. I had no problem with him. I just did not want a football coach to be our athletic director. It was not a good fit.

Not long after, Tom did get fired for something that was not his fault. He kept an assistant on staff as an unpaid advisor, more of a goodwill gesture than anything else. Coach Lou helped with the kickers. He insisted kickers approach the ball straight on and kick it with a square toe shoe. The method was outdated. Football place kickers had been using a soccer style approach for years. But Lou was a former University of Minnesota player from bygone days and the players liked him.

From what I understand Lou was leaving the stadium one Saturday after a bad defeat when he saw President Gavin. He shouted, "This is all your fault." It was quite embarrassing. Tom was fired the next day.

Little did we know how much better off the department would have been if Tom stayed on as head football coach. He was a good coach. He knew how to get the most from Macalester players. He could recruit. That was not the case with his immediate successors.

STREET SMARTS.

I made friends around campus in a strategic way. I worked closely with admissions and financial aid. I was already friends with Jimm Crowder, the international student admissions counsellor, and the only real friend of Macalester athletics in his department. Two more friendships emerged in a different way.

Geography professor David Lanegran asked to meet me for a drink one night. David really wanted to meet with me because two of his geography students Matt and Roger, my New Zealanders, had extolled my virtues to him. He needed to meet the man his prize students admired.

We arranged to meet at a bar, and he brought with him David Busse the financial aid director. They were good friends. We enjoyed each other's company and a real friendship developed. We met on a regular basis and talked about a variety of college affairs. I asked Dave how financial aid worked. I found out Macalester was one of the more prestigious academic schools that provided one hundred per cent of need-based aid. That helped me recruit a top player I saw at a recruiting showcase. I wrote to Larry Griffin and we started the recruiting process. He applied and was admitted. Then he received his financial aid award. Since he came from a very poor family, the award covered virtually all his college expenses.

When I contacted him, he told me he was grateful for the generous award, but he could not afford the loan. Though his aid package amounted to almost a full ride in aid, it included a loan of about two thousand dollars. I immediately went to work.

I approached our athletic liaison at Mac because I was not allowed to talk directly with a financial aid officer. The liaison told me the aid package was extremely generous and could not be increased. I went to great lengths to explain to him what real poverty was.

I told him how I would not have gone to college because my parents could not afford it, and how much that scholarship meant to me. When you are the first in your family to go to college, the family does not understand the advantages of a college education, and they are not interested in loans. I told him that this was the case for this player's family. The only thing they could see was the debt. My argument resonated. A revised offer from our financial aid department meant he enrolled.

MEN AND WOMEN IN THE SAME SEASON?

In 1988, the year before I took over my new position, the women's team finished sixth in the MIAC with a record of 2-5-1. We improved dramatically in my first year. We won our first seven games and finished third in the conference. Three teams, including Macalester were selected for the NCAA playoffs.

I think Ken felt a little embarrassed by the turnaround, but I explained how he had recruited and coached the team well. The difference was all about one positional change. I moved his outstanding player Corie Curtis from sweeper to forward and explained my reasoning to Ken.

Corie was a speedster. If we could get the ball forward to her, she could run with it and give our defense a break. Keeping her forward would force our opponents to keep a few of their players back. Keeping her at sweeper, where Ken played her, meant the ball would always be around our goal. It was a defensive strategy, but it worked until I could do more coaching and recruit better players.

We hosted the regional round on the first playoff weekend and lost to UCSD 0-1 in overtime. What irony! Macalester lost to the team I last coached and, as with my men the year before, UCSD proceeded to go on and win the national championship. Though we did lose in the playoffs, I had an easy time of it in my first year as coach of the men's and women's teams. The Macalester men failed to make the playoffs.

In 1990 both teams earned bids to the national tournament. The good news for me was the women's championship started a week before the men's championship. Our women pulled off a huge upset by defeating UCSD in the first game, but we unfortunately lost to St. Ben's in the regional final.

The loss created no conflict for me. It freed me to coach the men the following weekend. We played an extraordinary game against St. Thomas. We totally dominated them but lost 0-1. I was disappointed. I also knew the time might come when both of my teams would compete in playoff games on the same weekend, resulting in a conflict I could not control.

However, in 1992, we graduated one of the finest classes of men's soccer players ever to play at Macalester and it started a playoff drought which lasted four years. It was not easy to continue to recruit outstanding players to Macalester, but in 1996 I put together another very good men's squad. The women's team lost a close playoff game to UCSD in 1992 and they found difficulty against a very good Gustavus team for the next few years.

I must mention my women's team manager Sheri Baker who graduated in 1994. She suffered a knee injury during her first year, but she stayed on as my manager.

I was glad to have her. She was a true team player and I could trust her. Not only was Sheri a good manager she became a great friend. One time after the first game of a tournament in Texas she accompanied me to the hotel bar. When the waitress asked to see her ID, the waitress did a double take. "Oh," she said, "I thought you were a boy." I never let Sheri forget it. Sheri and I have become lifelong friends and she helped me enormously later in my life when tragedy struck. My son and her son are good friends, and I know she is still there for me if I ever do need some help.

Sheri Baker now Sheri Halvorson, a wonderful help to me during difficult times.

Another story from this time is worth telling. We were at St. Bens when Heather Craig, one of our defenders, went down with what looked like a serious injury. The athletic trainers thought she might have broken a leg or an ankle, so they called an ambulance and she was transported to the St. Cloud hospital.

When we finished playing, I was faced with a dilemma. We had travelled to the game in two vans. While the players showered and dressed, I drove one of the vans to the hospital to check on Heather. Once I determined her status I could figure out if she came home with us.

My hair had started thinning and it always seemed to be windy at St. Bens. I have been plagued by conjunctivitis since I was a child, and my eyes always become bloodshot and red in the wind. I looked a mess when I arrived at the hospital. Evidently the first nurse I approached to ask where I could find Heather thought I looked a mess, too. She took one look at me and said "Detox. Turn left and go all the way down the hall." She was very embarrassed when I told her my reason for being there.

Heather Craig.

In 1996 the women played in a four-team regional in Chicago, on the weekend before the men were likely to play in the opening round of their tournament. I was not sure how I would manage a playoff weekend when both of my teams would play. Though we beat a good Heidelberg team in the first game, we lost in the regional final to the host team, the University of Chicago. If we had won, it might have been possible to host both the men's and the women's games on the following weekend, because the women's team would only play one game, the quarter final, with the winner going on to the next weekend and the Final Four.

In the same year I was involved in a crazy experience with the men. We had finished second to Concordia and were scheduled to play them at home in a four-team regional playoff. The first game between Luther and UCSD was set to kick off at 11:00 am Saturday morning, with the second game to follow. But we had a big problem. When the teams arrived at

Macalester stadium for the first game, the field was covered in snow. It was frozen underneath and the ball would not roll in the snow. Nobody really knew what to do.

The Luther coach said he had called home, and the weather was fine. Decorah, Iowa was three hours from the twin cities. It was feasible to drive there and play the games, but we had to act immediately in order to do it. The problem was that we needed NCAA permission to change sites and no one was available.

The weather was getting warmer where we were, so we decided to give it a go. The game kicked off and our team watched. It was quite humorous as the snow dramatically affected the quality of play, especially since the ball kept stopping when it gathered snow. As the game continued the players trampled down the snow, and as the weather warmed the snow started to melt. The extremely difficult playing conditions evened the playing field and took away any skill advantage one team might have. In the end Luther came out on top. Almost all the UCSD players were from California. They were visibly upset. They did not understand the financial aspect which dictated where the games were played.

Both teams had succeeded in destroying most of the snow, but it had started raining and conditions deteriorated even more. The rain was getting heavier and the water had nowhere to go because the ground was frozen. There were puddles on the field as we kicked off our game against Concordia.

The puddles got bigger as the game went on until it became farcical. Players tried to lift the ball with their feet to volley it to gain distance. The ball would not roll. By the time I talked to the team at half time in the locker room I was soaked to the skin, and so were my players.

The game was tied at the end of regulation.

We went inside for ten minutes before beginning the overtime. I remember standing fully clothed under a hot shower. I was so wet it did not matter, I needed warmth. No one scored in overtime and Concordia won the shootout. They lost to Luther the next day.

The absurd conditions we experienced that day very likely contributed to a change in NCAA policy. In the future an NCAA representative was appointed to oversee each site during playoffs. The representative was a neutral party, usually someone from the regional committee.

I never thought I would say that the NCAA made a good decision about implementing rules, but the representative proved helpful, as there were times when coaches disagreed or did not understand the protocol. Most importantly, the representative had a way to contact the NCAA if a critical decision had to be made, like moving a site from St Paul to Decorah. We really could have used a representative on that snowy rainy day.

SUCCESS MAKES IT MORE DIFFICULT.

Both teams were very successful in the latter half of the 1990's. Friday night games not only helped me to coach both teams, but winning teams attracted large crowds to home games. Friday night games served as an end of the week celebration for our students. They were loud and sang obnoxious songs. This created a great atmosphere which equipment manager Ron Osterman kept under control. I knew our players loved to play in front of them and our fan support certainly helped with recruiting.

The 'gigolo'. Both teams acknowledged our crowd at the end of games with this dance.

I still needed the help of opposing coaches to switch regularly scheduled Saturday games to Friday nights so I could coach both teams. One or two coaches started to balk. By not agreeing to the switch I think they thought they could gain an advantage.

One men's coach did not wish to change the game date. I believe he wanted to play on Saturday because we would not have such a large crowd and I would have to choose to coach either the men's or the women's game. He said that my coaching both teams was my problem. I pointed out that when we played a midweek game at his college, we had to miss class by playing in the afternoon because his field did not have lights. I really irked him when I suggested that we should ask his players. His field was located at the edge of campus and attracted very few spectators. I knew opposing players loved playing in our noisy stadium in front of a raucous crowd. He did not take my suggestion and we continued to play his team at home on a Friday night.

A much more insidious incident demonstrated that our winning teams had upset the apple cart. There were two men's head coaches who had worked together at another MIAC school as head coach and assistant. The assistant landed the head coaching job at another college in the MIAC. They were good friends and schemed together before our standard end of season coaches meeting. They made an appalling proposal: an American born player must win the MIAC player of the year award. Foreign students were exempted.

I responded quickly. The idea was absurd. It was clearly discriminatory and obviously aimed at one school. I said the award would not be as significant if some of the best soccer players in the conference were not eligible for it. I also reminded them that the resumes of three of our players, Mick Hindes, Armin Heuberger and Matt Highfield, were sent to all coaches around the country by recruiting agencies. "Who will be next?" I asked.

I knew this question would anger another coach in the room because I was hinting about racial discrimination. Denzil Lue, the St. Thomas coach was Jamaican. He had a bitter rivalry with the pair of proposing coaches. We were friends and he immediately spoke up. He said "Yes, who will be next?" The idea went no further.

Below appears a photograph of our 1998 team. The names, and the countries of our international players are included in the caption.

1998 Team.

Back row L to R. 1, Roger Bridge, asst coach New Zealand, 3, Kimani Williams, Jamaica, 4, Armin Heuberger, Germany, 5, Erik Mykletun, Norway, 7, Mario Huck, Argentina, 8, Kjetil Storaas, Norway, 11, Roland Broughton, New Zealand, 12, Martin Oppenheimer, Sweden, 13, John Leaney, coach, England. Front row. 1, David Salmon, England, 3, Gabe Carvalho, Brazil, 6, Shingai Mukurazita, Zimbabwe.

I think this ploy was born out of desperation. The proposing coach's teams had enjoyed success. They viewed what they thought of as Macalester's endless supply of overseas players as a real threat. Macalester was not the only college in Minnesota with international connections. Augsburg had a relationship with Scandinavian countries. St. Olaf had a Norwegian player for one year, who was the best player I had ever seen in the MIAC. Many overseas students were available to most colleges. Recruiting agencies sent their literature to all colleges. I used this resource as well. I was quick to point out another disadvantage to the MIAC group. Macalester had highly selective admission standards and would not admit students who could gain entrance to all the MIAC colleges, except Carleton.

THE GOLDEN YEARS.

The six seasons between 1997 and 2001 could easily be called the best run for both our men's and women's teams. The men won or shared the MIAC title in five of the six years. The women won five straight titles and then finished third during a season when they did not surrender a goal. They were defensive specialists and conceded only five goals in conference play over a six- year period.

While there was acrimonious debate regarding our enrollment of male international players, the women had an even better record with only a little overseas assistance. My ability to coach both teams in playoffs was being stretched. I knew it was not going to be long before the women made the quarter final round and their match would be played on the weekend, when the men played their regional games. In 1997, it finally happened. It was the second week of November. It was cold in Minnesota. It could snow at any moment. I knew we had little chance of hosting a home playoff game. Then the women won their regional in Chicago and advanced to a Saturday quarter final game at Washington University in St Louis Missouri. Their game unfortunately conflicted with the men's opening round game in Thousand Oaks, California.

I checked the schedule and discovered our women were slated to play an evening game. Then to my consternation I understood the reasoning behind scheduling an evening game in November. Washington University's football team was scheduled to play a regular season game that afternoon on the same grass field. The football game would rip up the turf and make playing good soccer a nightmare. The wear and tear on a game field used by two soccer teams and a football team was the reason Macalester installed a synthetic field. So, here is the bottom line: an NCAA women's soccer playoff game was playing second fiddle to a regular season football game. I was appalled.

I called the NCAA and raised my concerns. I was disappointed that a regular season football game was awarded priority over a women's NCAA playoff game. I reminded them about 'Title Nine' and insinuated that some athletic administrators continued to live in the past. They viewed women's sport as second class. I demanded action, saying the field would be atrocious, and would ruin a quarter final regional championship game.

I was delighted when the NCAA acted and moved the game to Friday evening. The women would have much better conditions to play their game, plus I could catch a Friday night red eye flight to California. The men kicked off at 11.00 a.m. Saturday.

Unfortunately, the women lost a very close game 1-2 to Wash U as they were known. I raced to the airport and flew to Los Angeles where I rented a car and drove out to Cal Lutheran University, the site of the men's regional. I arrived a half an hour before the kickoff. We defeated Colorado College 2-0. The next day we played Cal Lutheran to a 0-0 regulation tie, and then played a scoreless overtime, only to lose in the shootout.

As our seasons ended, I realized how lucky I had been up until this point. I began to wonder if coaching both teams was going to present a similar scenario in years to come. Though Macalester's senior administrators might have been pleased by the success of the soccer teams, they did not truly seem to care. If they did, I would have been permitted to hire a full-time assistant for each team. Of course, Football had a full-time assistant, even as they remained the doormat of the MIAC. On the other hand, our soccer teams thrived in a nationally regarded conference, one that typically qualified two or three teams for the NCAA tournament.

CAN WE WIN A NATIONAL CHAMPIONSHIP?

Both teams in 1998 were capable of winning Macalester's first soccer national championship. But which one? This was the year I finally realized that the problem of a potential playoff coaching conflict might come to a head, especially when the men and women both won their conference championships, albeit the men shared theirs.

I believed the women could make a good run in the playoffs. The regional was scheduled in Illinois at Wheaton College, where we beat a tough Gustavus team 1-0 in overtime. The win set up a revenge match against the only team to defeat us in the regular season, the University of Chicago. The Wheaton College staff filmed the game. Only later when I watched the film did I hear their reaction to the best goal I have ever seen in college soccer.

Tawni Epperson,
Division III National Player of the Year 1998.

In the second half senior Tawni Epperson picked the ball up in her own half and set off on a determined run. She beat several defenders before going around the Chicago keeper and tapping the ball into the net. The press box staff raved about the play. I will never forget their reaction, and I smile every time I watch the replay.

The women were through to the quarter final, and we earned home field advantage and a chance to play Washington University. The men won a midweek game at Luther. I was pleased with both results, but I knew it was going to complicate the coming weekend for me.

I was dismayed when I learned that the men were sent to play at Pacific University in Oregon, while on the same day the women were scheduled for a home game. This time I could find no solution. Should I travel to Oregon with the men or stay home with the women? The solution was quite simple. Roger Bridge had played for me. Now he was my men's assistant. He had been by my side the whole season and knew all the players. I trusted him completely. Since I was not in the habit of changing the starting line-up, or the tactics, his main responsibility would be to make substitutions. I knew he could do that.

In their first game in Oregon the team avenged a regular season loss to St. Olaf with a 1-0 win. I talked on the phone with Roger after the game and he was satisfied.

The second game was far more problematic. When I talked with him later, he was very emotional. We had beaten a good team, Pacific University, on their own field, but Roger explained we played most of the game with ten men. He told me that our very good forward Larry Griffin had been sent off early in the game for a foul Roger could not explain. I later saw the video and it was a ridiculous decision. The opposing goalkeeper collected the ball, and as Larry was taking a route away from him the goalkeeper inexplicably jumped in his way. Larry was very strong and in the collision the keeper was flattened. Larry was ejected. It was a ridiculous decision.

Lack of play off funding was one of the problems that plagued the early years of all NCAA Division III tournaments, and this directly affected the selection of officials. Rather than flying in more competent referees the NCAA assigned officials from a local pool. The officials for the Macalester v Pacific game were local. They had seen Pacific play. They had officiated some of their regular season games. This familiarity probably biased the call against Larry. The bottom line was Larry was suspended for the next game, which is the reason Roger was so distraught. Regardless of the decision, the team victory meant the men would play a quarter final game the next weekend.

We had the same situation with assigning officials for our Minnesota playoff games. This was not unusual. Only later, after many complaints, and the addition of money from the television rights to the Division I basketball tournament, did the NCAA alter its policy. But that did not help Larry. The men were through to the quarter final game the next weekend, but unfortunately Larry would miss the game through suspension.

While this fiasco was going on in Oregon, the women played a home quarter final against Washington University. It was cold and we matched up against a team who I thought had more individual talent.

The game was tightly contested. It took four overtimes and a shoot out to determine a winner. For a change we emerged victorious and we were going to the final four. I was pleased for all my players. Both teams were now still alive in the playoffs, but their success posed more problems for me. I was faced with an impossible situation. I could not coach both teams next weekend. It just could not be done. I chose the women and here is my reasoning.

Later, some of the men were to indicate there was some sort of preference, after I had previously stayed home with the women, as opposed to traveling with the men. My reasons for choosing to go with the women were not based on a preference for a team. The women's tournament had advanced to the final four while the men were scheduled to play a quarter final game. Logically then, the women were one step closer to a national championship than the men. They were much closer to bringing a national championship back home, something no other team from Macalester had ever accomplished.

I had another problem, however. A big one. Roger the men's assistant was to be married the same weekend as these games were scheduled to be played. He could not travel with or coach the men. I needed to send our junior varsity coach John Curtis, who had only occasionally watched the team from the sidelines.

I was of course concerned, but I knew the men's team was immensely talented. They did not need much coaching. They were skilled individual players, and they played with an abandon I very often encouraged. The only problem would be making the right substitutions. It was a good problem to have, however. Our team had virtually eighteen starters. The only stumbling block was that John did not know their talent the way I did. He did not truly understand the potential impact each player could have on a game. He would not know how, or if, some of these talented substitutes could change a game if we were tied or losing. Nevertheless, I was confident in him. My decision to leave John in charge was also affected by the fact my assistant for the women, Steve Bellis had only been with me for one year.

The women's team was nearly as talented. We had some exceptional players and outstanding speed at forward. However, we had some role players on the team. We had already beaten a more talented team in Wash U, but I was sure we would face some very strong teams in the Final Four, and that coaching tactics would be crucial. I knew the women would be extremely disappointed if I did not coach them. The right decision was made.

When I heard the result of the men's game I was crushed. They had lost in the third overtime to the home team Greensboro College 1-2. I was crushed because the game was so close, and we did not have Larry Griffin. The fact they played three overtimes meant the substitutions were indeed critical. To make matters worse, Greensboro proceeded to win their semifinal game, before losing a close game in the final. In other words, the Macalester men were clearly good enough to win the title. Could I have made that much difference? Who knows? I might have coached them and lost the game by more. Such is soccer and coaching.

My decision however was completely justified when the women played their semifinal game against Willamette University. Willamette were an extremely well coached team, and after we scored a surprise goal early, they dominated the action. At the half time break I made quite probably the most critical coaching decision of my career.

I normally did not like the fact half time breaks had lengthened to fifteen minutes. I much preferred shorter breaks, but this time I needed fifteen minutes.

I used this time to convince my team to adopt a defensive strategy which was the very opposite of the strategy I had employed for years. My teams were coached to push the opposition wide, away from the middle, where they would not be as dangerous. In this game Willamette were dominating us with their wide play, and it was only a matter of time before they scored. I had fifteen minutes at half time to convince my players to do the opposite of what they had been taught to do for years.

I had complete faith they would try to do what I asked. I also understood that I would be criticized if we lost. But in making this decision I justified my reason for choosing to coach the women's team. No assistant, whether they believed it was the right move or not, would dare make such a major strategy change, it was too risky.

The change worked. Instead of attacking down the middle Willamette kept recycling to the outside, as they were coached. The change confused them, and we held on for a 1-0 win. We would play for the national championship the next day.

NATIONAL CHAMPIONSHIP.

I watched The College of New Jersey defeat the home team Ithaca College 2-0 in the other semifinal. I am sure they watched us too. Though they looked like a very good team I was not one to alter our game plan because of the opposition. The strategy change against Willamette was an exception. I taught my players to play our game and react to situations as they occurred. In that respect I had some very intelligent players on our team. We kept to that strategy.

New Jersey had an All-America forward and we played man marking at the back, so I told Laura Neumann, the quicker of our two central markers, to make sure she closely marked this player. Laura played an outstanding game. In fact, everybody played above their ability, which they needed to do, to compete with a team familiar with winning national titles.

I have a theory as to how the game unfolded. New Jersey played a very physical game and did it with a nasty attitude. They pulled jerseys and fouled a lot. It was clearly a strategic tactic, and I wonder if it was planned.

One time I watched a Jersey player offer the ball to our player for a throw in, and as our player went to take the ball, the Jersey player shoved it in her chest. Here is my theory.

Before every game our team had a ritual. They sang loudly 'Come on Eileen' from Dexy's Midnight Runners. They were singing it in the parking lot when New Jersey arrived, and their team looked on in amazement. I have always believed some coaches over think their strategy. I believe their coach thought we were a simple mid-west team, who were not seriously competitive players. He watched us sing and coached his team to try to intimidate the simple midwestern girls. It backfired.

Their coach also 'played politics.' Before the game he objected to the selection of officials. I did not know any of them because they were from the east coast. He apparently did. I think he was pleased, when after voicing his objection, the NCAA settled on the third or fourth choice, the only female referee. I believe he thought his players could now get away with more fouling and intimidating play. He could not have been more wrong she worked an excellent game.

New Jersey dominated possession but our dangerous speed on the break always posed a threat. Their petty fouling and antics irritated our players, but we kept our game plan and played them to a 0-0 tie in regulation. I am proud of my speech during the break before overtime.

My team whined about their treatment from the opposition and about their petty fouling and nasty behavior. I raised my voice and gave what I consider to be one of my best talks.

"Listen, all of you. We will read the result in the paper tomorrow. The article will not mention New Jersey's foul play or their petty and nasty tactics. It will not say they intimidated you. It will, however, show the result. Now get over it and fight back. Remember the only thing we will see in the paper or the history book is the result."

Early in the fourth overtime, Tawni Epperson did what she had done in Chicago. She took a ball and beat several players, finally pushing it past the opposing keeper.

Every player on our team immediately piled on her. I remember saying to Steve my assistant, "We did it, we did it, against all the odds." The player's parents who had travelled over a thousand miles rushed the field and joined the celebration.

Tawni Epperson scoring the winning goal.

**Tawni with, a hug for her coach, along with Anna Bacho our keeper.
Salli, Tawni's mother is in the background.**

We hardly had time to celebrate anything. Four overtimes had cut short the time we needed to drive to the airport.

The team literally piled into the vans and we took off for Syracuse airport.

The flight home was memorable, as was the reception when we arrived back. Several of the team's boyfriends, fans and parents greeted us at the terminal. I believe there may have been a party that night.

Macalester Women's Soccer

Macalester College
1998 NCAA Division III National Champions

For my sins I was voted National Coach of the Year for 1998. I am pictured below with the Division One recipient.

SPONSORSHIP.

My friend RJ Anderson alerted me to sponsorship. I was aware that some coaches made deals with sporting goods companies so that coaches and players could be seen wearing a company's line of clothing. RJ was obsessed. He wanted to garnish his coaching wardrobe free of charge, and he wanted to be sponsored by a sporting goods company. Ultimately, he became a Division I coach in Toledo Ohio, and did negotiate some agreements with companies who wanted teams to play in their apparel.

A few years before we won our national championship, I had worked extensively with the National Sports Center in Blaine, Minnesota. It was to promote the USA Cup as a tournament for college coaches to attend and identify recruits. It did not work out particularly well because the organizing committee was more interested in creating the largest youth soccer tournament in the country, which it did. Unfortunately to do this it also lowered the standard of soccer. College coaches did not consider it a major tournament worth attending.

Umbro Sporting Goods, an English football and sportswear company, was one tournament sponsor, and we agreed to a clothing contract. If RJ had my contract, he would have filled his wardrobe with clothing related attire. I did not take advantage. I merely acquired enough to appear in Umbro attire every time I went out.

During the summer I worked with the USA Cup. The player considered by many as the greatest player ever, Pele, came to the Blaine tournament. His contract with Umbro obliged him to attend the largest youth tournament in the world. I was invited to an event called 'Dinner with Pele.'

After we won our championship wearing Umbro jerseys, the company stopped doing business in the US. I was left without a sponsor. I heard about an Italian company that distributed a wide variety of athletic clothing and shoes. Diadora was looking for ways to promote their products.

It was the summer after our national championship, and I told them we had not yet taken a formal team photograph to celebrate our achievement. They jumped at the offer and immediately approved it.

**Here I am with the great man. The person in between us is the
Umbro rep. I know nobody else.**

I stayed with Diadora for the rest of my coaching career, and I believe I was good value. A nationally distributed soccer-centric newspaper 'Soccer America,' promoted a coaching panel at tournaments all over the country, and I was very often invited as the Division III representative. I participated in these panel discussions with Division I coaches wearing my Diadora attire. I still have my favorite Diadora sweats.

REPEAT.

In 1999 both teams each lost three important starters to graduation. I recruited three outstanding men who did in fact fill their places. In the women's team our senior class was extraordinary, and the first years had seasoned as they watched from the bench and saw spot duty. The women remained nationally competitive.

The men won the conference with a 9-0-1 record and only conceded three goals. The women produced another outstanding season and went undefeated in MIAC play without conceding a goal. In the home regional they trounced Simpson 5-0. They scored a 2-0 victory over the University of Chicago, to gain a now familiar place in the quarter final. Once again, I feared I would face a scheduling conflict. This time I was lucky.

The men traveled to Wheaton College in Illinois for their regional. Wheaton is a devoutly Christian school and does not compete on Sundays. Consequently, the regional was scheduled for Friday and Saturday. Since the women's quarter final was a single game, we scheduled it for Sunday.

The men lost to a very good UW Oshkosh team and were eliminated. On Sunday the women hosted North Carolina Wesleyan and won a tightly contested game 1-0. We were headed back to the Final Four.

We defeated Williams College 1-0 and faced UCSD in the final. It was the fourth time in five years that UCSD had reached the final. The previous year they were knocked out by St. Benedict of the MIAC, a team coached by my very good friend Bill Kelly, who played soccer at Macalester back in the day. I thanked him often and told him I am sure he contributed to our national title with that result. As an alum he was proud to help.

Holly Harris (5) and Kate Ryan Reiling (10)
Two All Americans.

The final was not a great game. As the underdogs, with pace up front, we counter attacked. UCSD scored early but then played defensively to hang on. With a few minutes to go there was an incident, and if I had not been friends with their coach Brian McManus, I think it might have escalated. His forwards dribbled the ball to the corner flag near our goal and stood on the ball to waste time.

I yelled at the ref because the NCAA had a rule called 'unsportsmanlike conduct.' The referee failed to heed my complaint, so I yelled at my players. "If the ref will not do anything, then take her out and take a yellow."

Brian looked at me.

I repeated my comment exactly and then turned to Brian, "If I were you, I would not encourage your players to do this, if you do not want a player hurt. Your team is too good to resort to this."

He called it off.

I shook hands and congratulated him after the game, and we are still friends. I still consider this play a scourge in soccer, and simply enforcing the unsportsmanlike conduct rule would put an end to it.

REFEREES.

I am obligated to mention the interaction I had with referees during my long coaching career. When asked later in my career what I thought of referees I said, "I like them, I married one."

If I had issues, and I had plenty, it typically resulted from my absolute problem with 'injustice,' whether it appears on the soccer field or in life. Few people understand the work a coach puts in, only to see a win or a loss decided by one critical decision. This does not happen frequently, but it is the fear of it happening that makes some coaches more volatile, and I could be accused of being one of them. Most referees did a very good job, but there are a couple of stories worth telling.

The best crew of referees I encountered were the three we saw at many of our Minnesota contests: Steve Cook, RJ Anderson, and my future wife Carrie Schulz. Because I coached both teams, I tried to arrange double headers when possible. We could do this at Macalester because we had floodlights. A crew of three officials would work both games. Early on, Steve and RJ served as center officials with Carrie on the line. Later, Carrie took the middle in many of the women's games. They were all excellent referees.

Steve was English and RJ was Scottish, so they both grew up playing the game and understood it well. Later when RJ became a coach, and we worked soccer camps together, he and I played on the same team in camp games. We were better players than the other coaches, and we consistently passed to each other to set up scoring situations. RJ was a much better player than me in his time. Carrie also grew up playing soccer at her high school in Minneapolis, and she played for a team her father coached.

One game this trio officiated stands out. We hosted St. Thomas in a NCAA playoff game, and RJ had the middle. We were pounding St. Thomas but could not score. Against the run of play RJ awarded St. Thomas a free kick, not far outside our penalty area. The kicker scored an excellent goal direct from the free kick. I had already sounded my disbelief of the free kick when it was awarded. I did not see a foul.

We threw everything at them from then on, until the final whistle, but we were ousted from the playoffs, and I was angry. I approached RJ afterwards and asked him about his call. He said he called a push to which I replied, "But you would not have given that as a penalty, if it was inside the penalty area."

He understood the inference. A good referee would not award a penalty for such an innocuous offense. I am sure he did not expect St. Thomas to score. There was also the possibility he tried to placate their coach, Denzil Lue. They had a volatile relationship and Denzil berated him from the sidelines most of the game.

We met in the bar as usual afterward, but I was late. RJ knew where I had been. He looked at me sheepishly and said, "You watched the film." I replied "Yes, you do not want to see the film." Long afterward we laughed at the situation because we were friends. It took a couple of years, but he finally asked to see the film. After viewing the play, he was slightly embarrassed, but he insisted it was a push, to which I again said, "But you would not give a penalty for that." I think he knew it was a mistake, but who would have thought they would score such a spectacular goal.

I did one thing that was different than most coaches. I never met with the players after a game. It is a time when emotions run high. I believed my comments at that time might do more harm than good. Besides, I could get a reality check by watching the film. I could objectively evaluate the game and my players performance. I would use the film session as an educational tool. Withholding my comments until after the game allowed me to relay my thoughts to the players in a constructive more thoughtful way, at a time when my words were not tarnished by emotion. I never blamed the officials for our defeats to the players either and I silenced them if they broached the subject. Bottom line; I tried to find ways of turning any loss into a learning experience.

I allowed my emotions to get the better of me in another home playoff game. This time it was a team visiting from California. Their coach constantly berated the referee and kept using phrases like "We came all the way from California to see this?" He was more than hinting that the mid-west referee, Tony Vasoli, was favoring the home team, which he most definitely was not.

The game went to penalty kicks. We led 3-1 in the shootout and it was their turn. If they did not score it was virtually over, because they kicked first. Our goalkeeper saved the kick, but Tony blew his whistle and claimed our keeper moved early, so the kick was to be retaken.

This rule was instituted to stop keepers from running out toward the kicker when the whistle blew. It was accepted that keepers would guess the direction the kicker would choose, and then would move early, but sideways. We quite often see this in professional soccer today. Some kickers anticipate the keeper's movement and simply chip the ball straight down the middle, to the place the keeper just vacated.

I understood the pressure situation of these kicks, and I had instructed my keeper not to dive early, but to wait. The real pressure was on the kicker. Nevertheless, the call was made. They scored the retake and we missed our next two. They did not miss another, and we lost the shootout 3-4.

Of course, I expressed my displeasure at the time and yelled from my position about fifty yards back. The officials knew I was angry. They showed they understood how angry I was when as soon as we missed our last kick they sprinted for the changing room. I tried in vain to sprint after them, but the pitch was invaded by the substitutes and coaches of the winning team, plus the fourth official succeeded in stopping me. The only explanation I can offer for the actions of an inexperienced official is by referring to a common definition of our home state 'Minnesota nice.' I think the official had listened to their coach complain all game the officiating crew were 'homers.' I believe he thought with the shootout going heavily in our favor, he would show a little Minnesota nice.

Once again, I was late to the bar. My assistants and many members of our athletic department who were at the game were waiting. They knew I had watched the film.

"His arm moved upwards, no other part of his body moved," was all I said. My assistants then explained to our staff how bad the referee's call had been.

Of course, I made many mistakes in my dealings with officials and if I knew them, as I did with our Minnesota officials, I was always prepared to apologize. I often did so before the next game, hoping to make them think I was a nice guy, for obvious reasons. I wanted the next close call to go our way.

Playing in small towns frustrated me because they tended to employ the same officials. Conversely, Macalester is situated in the Twin Cities, which is home to six MIAC schools. Another four are located not much more than an hour away. We had access to more officials, and they moved around.

Stevens Point, Wisconsin is the perfect example of a small-town venue. We saw the same referee each time we visited.

He was so familiar with the home side that he unconsciously favored them by awarding them the benefit of the doubt. Say for instance he watched a home team girl make a dubious challenge to a player on the ball. He would typically think *I know her; she did not mean to make that dangerous play*, and not blow his whistle. It made for an unfairly officiated game.

Later I had an idea that I think worked. When I was a member of the NCAA regional committee, part of my job was to find referees for the play off sites. I usually asked for local assistance and I remember asking the referee from Stevens Point if he wanted to be included, saying I would recommend him. After he happily accepted, I made a point of talking to him at the site. I reminded him I considered him competent enough to officiate an important national playoff game. It was a backhanded attempt to remind him to make judicious calls, plus it was a compliment as well.

Ironically, the next time we played at Stevens Point I noticed their coach having a go at him after the game. Maybe his performance was a little fairer, this time.

Another time in Chicago, I was so frustrated with the officiating I complained enough to cause the official to walk towards me and address the issue. As he approached me, I impulsively said, "If you are coming to give me a yellow card, it might be the first correct call you have made all game." As soon as the words left my mouth, I wanted to take them back. If I were in his position I would have responded with "In that case I will give you a red card." I was fortunate. He merely told me to sit down which I did. I continue to respect officials who can accept criticism without resorting to red cards.

I remember another game in Chicago when I was once again unhappy. It was a big playoff game and there was a large crowd. Many fans crowded behind the team bench because there was no other place to stand. They were about three or four rows deep. I was shouting at the referee because I felt we were being unfairly treated and wondered aloud if the referee was familiar with the home side.

It is quite possible, due to the size of Chicago, that various suburbs had their own local referees. The official grew tired of my complaints. He blew the whistle, halted the game and began walking in my direction. He was a long way from me in the other half of the field. I stepped back and hid myself in the crowd. The fans around me just stared in disbelief.

He approached our bench and looked for me. I am certain he knew what I looked like because I had harassed him for a while. However, he stopped when he could not find me and returned to the game. As I stepped out of the crowd and returned to the sideline, I said out loud, "I suppose I had better behave myself now."

NCAA TOURNAMENT SELECTION.

Throughout my career, I participated on NCAA regional ranking and tournament selection committees. A small portion of the enormous contract the NCAA signed with CBS to televise the Division I men's basketball tournament filtered down to Division III, and it allowed for the expansion of Division III national tournaments. The soccer tournament expanded, and some conferences received one guaranteed tournament entry. Then various selection committees determined the 'at large' entries to complete the brackets.

The automatic bid guarantee created a problem at all levels but especially at Division III. Quite frankly some Division III conferences did not deserve automatic bids, especially when it excluded stronger teams who participated in more competitive leagues. Our easy 5-0 victory over Simpson in the 1999 women's tournament is a prime example of this disparity. Simpson College played in a weak conference and earned a playoff spot by the virtue of the automatic bid. The same thing happened all over the country. Strong teams were omitted because they had not won their conference, and there was no more room in the field for them.

The NCAA played catch up by continually expanding the tournament until we reached sixty-four teams. Then all conferences were awarded an automatic qualifier. The big question centered on the number of available 'at large' places, and who would be selected.

Strength of schedule remained the key element in selecting teams from all over the country for at large bids. Though the size of the tournament did change, this had been the prime determining factor.

It was calculated after all teams were assessed a power rating on a scale from one, as the strongest, to five as the weakest. A formula was created where a team was awarded a strength of schedule index, which was formed by adding together the power rating of each team on a team's schedule and dividing by the number of games played. It was a little more complicated than that, but the bottom line was that 'at large' teams were chosen by a committee, whose decisions were always criticized by the coaches, players and fans of the excluded teams.

One story comes to mind. A coach from a team with a strong winning record, in a very weak region, complained to me that the whole process had been rigged for years. All because his team had previously not been selected.

Later, after all Division III conferences received automatic bids, and this same coach's team finally qualified, he harangued me with, "Now you will see how wrong you were all these years." His team lost 0-9 in the first game, and of course I never heard from him again.

Once we had reached sixty-four teams the whole tournament saw less complaining. If you were not one of the best sixty-four teams in the country, you did not have the right to complain.

The CBS money helped in other ways too. Now if more than one team from the same conference was selected, instead of playing each other in the first round, the selection committees would do their best to split up conference opponents. It meant more travel, but we all wanted to avoid each other, as it lessened the experience for the players.

Most conferences around the country complete their season with conference play offs. The NCAA mandated the automatic qualification must go to the playoff winner, not the winner of the regular season competition. MIAC coaches wanted to initiate a playoff format. I was not in favor.

When it was first proposed at a soccer coaches meeting, I was strongly against it. I could not for the life of me understand why the team that emerged victorious in our conference, after ten hard fought games, would basically be subjected to a lottery, as the conference playoffs would be, in November on icy fields.

I argued in a nasty tone. I said I would never believe just finishing in the top four was good enough. I believed in playing to win. We would never back down. We started every season with the goal of winning the conference in the regular season. "If you are voting for this", I said "you are saying you are playing for fourth place. You are trying to make the NCAA playoffs by the back door, because you do not believe you can win the conference."

For two straight years my argument prevailed, and a vote was not called. The third time it was proposed, I produced the same argument. I waited for a reply and the room remained silent. "Oh, I see, by not engaging in dialogue with me it means you met together before this meeting. You do not think you can produce an argument strong enough to counter mine, so you are not going to comment." There was silence. No one responded. Then somebody called for a vote. They voted it in.

There is an incredible irony to all this. The first year the MIAC conducted conference soccer playoffs, our women did not win the conference championship. We proceeded to win the playoff and earn the automatic bid, so we advanced to the national tournament. I thought it wise not to raise this issue at any future meetings.

THE TIMES THEY ARE A CHANGING.

We had excellent teams when a new president Michael McPherson succeeded Bob Gavin. We did not know it at the time, but his appointment signaled a change in athletics. The financial policies he implemented restricted our growth. Macalester no longer competed financially for students in the home market. To make matters worse, international student applications were primarily evaluated by the ability of the family to pay the full rate. McPherson did not care for athletics the way president Gavin did.

In recruiting we relied on hard work and the fact we had earned a reputation as a nationally known Division III soccer power. The men's team continued to attract international players, but they were now students who already planned to attend Macalester. Occasionally we admitted a good player, but I could no longer reliably recruit highly competitive players.

I was more than aware of the problems facing our teams if both squads made the playoffs, so I started delegating more responsibility to my assistants. When the new millennium arrived, we continued to be successful, but I knew coaching two teams was too much.

Steve Bellis was still my women's assistant, but he eventually moved on to become head coach at Concordia University in St. Paul.

I was extremely lucky on the men's side. Ian Barker had been a Division I assistant, when he moved to Minnesota to be the state coaching director for youth soccer. I heard he was available, so I contacted him. He had seen us play because we played the best college soccer in the Twin Cities.

The University of Minnesota, the only Division I university in the state, does not sponsor men's soccer. Ian was an outstanding coach and we hit it off immediately.

I delegated more and more responsibility to him. Then, in 2003, my life changed dramatically.

CARRIE.

In the early nineties, we played many Friday evening men's and women's double headers, and we used the same crew to officiate both games. Steve Cook and RJ Anderson took the middle of each game and at first David Dow ran the line. When David asked for more middle assignments, a young woman named Carrie Schulz became the third member of the crew. She was clearly assigned to this crew to learn the profession by observing, in my opinion, the two best officials in the MIAC.

I mentioned before Steve was from England and RJ was from Scotland, so we hit it off immediately. After the Friday games we headed to a local bar and discussed the game. Carrie accompanied us and sat and listened. I asked her one time why she came out with us. She said, "I like listening to you guys, but somebody has to get these men home."

It was not long before Carrie took the middle for a women's game, so RJ and Steve could critique her. She developed into a very good referee. Her father was from Germany and had coached youth soccer. He had introduced her to officiating at a young age, so she already knew the game.

Carrie was a good high school athlete, where she played volleyball, basketball and soccer. I remember a time when she was running the line on our side of the field, and for a moment she was stationary in front of our players. I thought I would have some fun. I said, "Do you want to go for a drink after the game?" My players thought I was hitting on her and immediately admonished me. She played along and replied, "Ok if you are buying."

What my players did not know was that I already planned to meet the officials in the bar after the game.

Carrie was fast tracked as a promising female referee.

The next year RJ and Steve showed up without Carrie. I asked about her and they told me she started a new job in Florida. I did not see her again for several years.

Then RJ decided to move to Panama, and he hosted a farewell party at a Minneapolis pub. When I arrived, Carrie was there. RJ was busy meeting and greeting many old friends, so Carrie and I found a corner and sat and talked. She had returned to the Twin Cities. She was working at the transplant medical facility. We exchanged phone numbers and e mail addresses.

Carrie at the National Championship at UCSD. Matt Adams, behind Carrie, had worked with me at UCSD. Strange coincidence, they did not know each other. He later helped me enormously with advice how to raise my son Jack, when I visited and stayed at his house.

I emailed a couple of times to inquire about her new job, and then I suggested we go for a drink and catch up. We really enjoyed each other's company. She told me about a friend of hers who was getting married soon, and would I like to be her guest at the wedding? It was held on a Saturday during the season, so I had a conflict. We were playing at St. Mary's and it was a two-hour drive back to Minneapolis. Since Carrie really wanted me to be there, we agreed I would miss the wedding but show up for the reception.

There were some men attending the reception who, I realized much later, were interested in dating Carrie. They were mostly acquaintances she had met at church activities. I later discovered that they were all interested to meet Carrie's new boyfriend. I arrived late, and of course I had come straight from a soccer game, so I was hardly dressed for a wedding reception.

Carrie was forty-two years old, but you would never know by looking at her. I was fifty-four and had lost most of my hair. Carrie greeted me when I arrived, and I received some strange looks from the men, as if they were saying to each other, "Him! She is dating him?" Clearly, I was older than most of the bride and groom's friends. Our age difference did not faze Carrie one bit. She proudly introduced me to all her friends. I was her new boyfriend.

Our relationship blossomed. Carrie said she always wanted to have children. She admitted that she had recently inquired about in vitro fertilization. Neither of us had been married before but we started to head in that direction. She asked if I ever wanted children. I replied honestly. I said I never really considered it before. But I started to think about it and decided I wanted to ask her to marry me. I summoned up the courage one night very late at a bar.

She answered in her typically direct manner. "Yes," she said, "I will marry you, but I want to be asked properly, not near midnight in some sleazy bar." It took me a while to think about where and when I could make a proper proposal. But there was one small hitch. She really wanted children and she believed I did not. "Where did you get that idea?" I asked. "When I asked you about children," she said, "you said you had never thought about it."

I looked at her and said "Yes, I had never thought about it, now I have, and I do want children. You will have to get used to the fact I say things exactly how I mean them." She was delighted. I formally asked her to marry me over dinner in a nice restaurant, she accepted. We were married at Central Lutheran Church in Minneapolis on June 5th, 2004. The church was Carrie's home church, the one she regularly attended with her mother.

**Wedding day back row left to right. Chris Price, Joanne Price, Alex Leaney, Michael Leaney.
Center, Wilford Schulz, Pat Price, Jan Leaney, Eero Schulz.
Front row Lillian Leaney, John, Carrie, Ardis Jacobson.**

It was a huge wedding with my family, plus a couple of college friends and their wives, coming from England. Carrie had an apartment in Lilydale, which had a beautiful view of the confluence of the Minnesota and Mississippi rivers. We decided to hold the reception there. It was a perfect setting, and more importantly Carrie adored the location.

Here is the view at the reception.

I WILL SEE YOU IN NOVEMBER.

After we married, Carrie's friends asked her about my frequent absences during soccer season. I traveled constantly, gone for weekends and out late after home games. She said to them "I told him I will see you in November."

Carrie did, in fact, attend every home game she could, and she traveled to some road games in the Twin Cities, too. She stayed in the background and waited until I was finished with the team. Many times, we went out for a drink after the game and she sat and listened, as my assistants and I broke the game down. She told me she really enjoyed it.

She also wanted children as soon as possible, as did I, after all I was no spring chicken. I well remember when she discovered she was pregnant. We were in a hotel on a break in Florida and I woke up to see her holding a pregnancy test a few inches from my face. I have no idea how long she had waited for me to wake. She was ecstatic. So was I.

I asked her if she wanted to know if we were having a boy or a girl. She did not want to know but I did. We were going to have a boy, but I kept it to myself.

In conversations I would occasionally refer to the baby as 'she' instead of the universal, 'he'. When I did, she looked at me and asked, "Is it a girl?"

I replied by saying I am just trying to even things out, trying to be equal, so you do not know. She would say later she thought we were going to have a girl because of the way I behaved.

On October 28th, 2004 she gave birth to our beautiful baby boy, whom we called Jack.

The only beautiful person in this photograph is Carrie.

I asked to christen him with the name John so he could later have a choice, as John can be called Jack. I have regretted this ever since, as he has always been Jack, and you cannot imagine the problems we have experienced. He and I are both officially named John A. Leaney, and when it comes to official business or producing the right insurance card, we have a problem. We gave him the middle name Albert, in honor of my Uncle Albert.

Carrie loved children. I have never seen anybody so happy as my beautiful wife with our baby Jack in her arms.

There is a funny story we often repeated when Carrie was asked about the number of boys and girls she wanted. She said she wanted four children, but because she had to give birth by C section, the doctors limited her to three. I had maintained all along I wanted two, a boy and a girl. When anyone asked Carrie whether she next wanted a boy or a girl, Carrie would always say "Another boy. That way I can get to three."

The christening.

Coaching both teams became too much of a burden for me, so we started a gradual transition with the men's team. Over the course of the next three years Ian and I worked together, until he became the sole head coach. Though admissions standards changed, and we could no longer rely on top class players, our teams remained competitive. We changed our recruiting strategy and emphasized our history as a nationally competitive team.

Apparently, President McPherson was not interested in competitive athletic teams, but a new president was on the horizon.

Ian is an outstanding coach. Eventually he brought the team into consideration as a contender for honors, but it was a struggle. We had always battled with several perennial rivals, St. Johns, St. Thomas, St. Olaf and Gustavus, for MIAC supremacy. But then Concordia and Carleton produced championship caliber teams, and the other conference teams were improving.

Carrie and I at a Middlesbrough game on her first trip to England to meet my friends.

It was much harder to win the conference, but Ian eventually achieved this, as did his successor Gregg Olson.

The women's team had been dominant and very little changed. From 1997-2006 they won seven MIAC titles, losing only four games, two of them in one season. I was only coaching one team, but life was to change.

WE FIGHT.

"Ouch," she said.

"What happened?" I asked, "Did he bite you?"

Carrie did not answer but she was breast feeding Jack when she felt the pain, and it was not a bite. Only later did I discover how much my life was going to change during the coming year.

"Mrs. Leaney, you have stage four breast cancer" the doctor said.

"What does that mean?" I asked. My wife looked at me and said, "It means we fight."

I had no idea at the time that stage four was considered terminal, and nobody told me. I was in above my head. There were so many things I did not know. I just wish a nurse or doctor had taken me aside and clearly explained the severity of her condition, and what we were in for.

Carrie knew about the medical world, she worked for a company that dealt with organ transplants. She knew how serious her condition was. She knew what stage four meant. When Carrie started chemotherapy a nurse finally explained to me that they were treating my wife with 'industrial strength' drugs. While I did not understand the medical term, this made sense. I brought Jack to visit.

As she weakened, Jack played on her bed, but he would not look at her or go near her. I apologized to Carrie, and reached for our son to admonish him, however Carrie understood. "He knows I cannot satisfy his needs" she said. After that, when we visited, I brought Jack into the room so Carrie could see him, and then asked a nurse to look after him.

The seriousness of Carrie's condition suddenly dawned on me. My wife was fighting for her life. It was apparent to everybody, including me, that the disgustingly strong chemo was not working. The doctors told me they were moving her to hospice.

What was hospice? How ignorant could I be? It soon became obvious.

I remember getting on her bed, crawling up where my face was close to hers, and telling her how much I loved her. I promised I would take care of Jack and devote my life to him.

Carrie died of metastatic breast cancer on September 29th, 2006.

LIFE GOES ON.

I was amazed by the number of people who offered help and support. My sister Pat and her husband Chris immediately flew over from England. It was the middle of soccer season and my assistants looked after the teams.

I lived in a haze. I remember the afternoon she died we had a game at Bethel College. I drove there and just wandered aimlessly in a nearby field, where I could watch the game, but I did not want to talk to anybody. Later in October the team traveled to Chicago and Pat and Chris came along to take care of Jack. I tried to ease the pain by immersing myself in my work.

The funeral took place at Central Lutheran Church in Minneapolis, the church she attended every Sunday with her mother. I will always remember seeing two of the nurses who looked after Carrie in the chemo ward at the funeral. Was this typical? Or was it because Carrie was so young and had a child? I was touched.

Two former players truly provided me with enormous help in those traumatic days. Grace King, a sophomore forward from Northampton Massachusetts, told me she had worked with young children when she was at high school. She offered to come and look after Jack during the day so I could carry on with my work. Sheri Baker, now Halvorson, who I mentioned earlier, also took Jack and cared for him at her house along with her son Erik, who was a few months older.

Carrie's parents lived apart. They were older and very distraught, not capable giving any real assistance, so the support that Grace and Sheri offered was invaluable.

I think they, along with almost everyone, understood that being with my team and helping them achieve their goals took my mind off the tragedy. It became obvious to Chris and Pat how much my team cared. The players were wonderful with Jack.

Grace King with Jack.

This traumatic season did not end the way we planned, and I was not surprised. There were so many distractions and coaching disruptions. The men lost six of their last eight games, and although the women went undefeated in the conference and made the playoffs, they ran into a very good Wheaton team and lost 0-3. Wheaton went on to win the national championship.

I had far more important things to consider.

Chris and Pat with Jack at my apartment.

A NECESSARY CHANGE.

There was no point in thinking I could continue as a college soccer coach. I was now a single parent with little help. I could not afford to spend so much time away from home and my son Jack. I needed to be fair to him. I started to think about how I could raise him and still work. I also needed the money.

I arranged a meeting with President Brian Rosenberg, and I asked if I could work part time and retain my benefits. I had worked for the college for over twenty years. Brian was very gracious.

He told me even though I technically held a 'staff position' that he would provide me with a faculty type deal. The college already dealt with aging faculty who did not want to retire by offering them a proposition. They had to design a project to complete over four years, with the caveat that they retire after that time. Brian promised to work out a similar deal for me and told me to consult with my athletic director, Travis Feezell. It in fact was left up to his successor Kim Chandler, as Travis left me alone knowing he was leaving.

I did not get along with my new boss. She would run the department in a dictatorial way. She drew up a plan for my part time employment and I showed it to my friend Ian.

He was puzzled, "How are you going to do all this?" he asked. I said, "I am not." I took a part of the plan that appealed to me and designed my own job description. I had earned that right. The best part of my new job was I reported to the president, not my athletic director. This was to be a huge source of discomfort to her.

I believed I could really help department members with the athletic recruiting process.

Macalester is a highly selective liberal arts college. The admissions department is committed to several principles in evaluating a candidate's admission. Though they consider many parameters, I understood that one of the primary qualifications they consider is what talents and skills the candidate can bring to the school.

My job was to look at each recruited athlete the way the admissions office would. I evaluated each set of qualifications and shared the recruit's likelihood of gaining admission with the coach. It made sense only to recruit student athletes with a strong chance of admission.

The admissions office gave me a book that listed all admitted students in the last five years, along with information about the respective academic strength of the high schools. Most importantly it showed the class ranking of students and where the admissions office had previously drawn the line at that school.

The information also included test scores. I learned to readjust the grade point average by striking out all non-academic subjects. In the end a candidate for admission was assigned a number with a plus or minus attached to it if necessary. This indicated whether the candidate could earn admission solely based on his or her academic record, or whether a coach needed to recommend the recruit for admission. This meant that sometimes a coach had to decide which candidates to support. A coach could only influence a few decisions. The sad thing for me was this college did not value this process of assisting athletes as much as its competitors did.

Though mathematics is my least favorite subject I became quite good at my job. I worked very hard to make sure that I completed any form sent to me on the same day I received it. I became quite adept at predicting the recruiting number that admissions would assign to athletic recruits. I am proud to say I was remarkably accurate. The best part of my new job was I reported to the president, not to my athletic director. This reporting structure became a huge source of discomfort to her.

After Grace graduated, I hired a woman to babysit Jack for the few hours a day I was at work, until he eventually went to kindergarten. Life was a little easier.

DIRECT OR BLOODY RUDE.

In a presentation I now commonly give, I open with the phrase "My friends say I am direct, and my enemies say I am bloody rude." If it is true it might have saved my life.

I have always felt it better to be 'up front' as they say. President McPherson once told a staff meeting of ours "If I want an opinion, I will ask John Leaney." So how did this save my life?

During my wife Carrie's battle with cancer, there were long periods when she was 'out of it' while undergoing chemotherapy. During this time, I talked to the nurses about many things, including the various forms of breast cancer. Carrie was afflicted with metastatic breast cancer which spread to her liver, and that is the primary reason she did not survive. The nurses told me men could also have breast cancer, something I did not know at the time.

One day I was rubbing what I thought was a mosquito bite on my chest that did not itch. I noticed a lump. It felt like a piece of gristle. I went to the doctor and asked him to examine me. After the examination he said "Mr. Leaney, I do not think you have breast cancer." His complacency irritated me, and I replied, "What kind of diagnosis begins with *I don't think?*" Do you think you could come up with a more definitive answer, rather than a diagnosis of *I don't think?*"

He was a little taken aback and said, "Well you would need an MRI to be sure." I responded immediately "I want to be sure, so can we set up the MRI?" Subsequent to the MRI the doctor looked very agitated. He said "Mr. Leaney, you have a grade three tumor and we need to operate as soon as possible."

The news stunned me, and my emotions were mixed. I was horrified by the discovery and relieved they had discovered it. So 'being direct or bloody rude' was a huge plus in the scheme of things. I quickly arranged to have the tumor removed. The operation was a complete success. Each time I go in to be checked the doctors tell me there is no need to return, that I am free and clear. I answer that I will return for a check-up every six months, and tell them, "You guys have been wrong before."

Every year Macalester holds a 'kick cancer' event at one of its home soccer games. I am the guest speaker at half time. I introduce my story with the phrase 'Am I direct or bloody rude?' On that day, I place on the front desk at the entrance to the stadium the picture below.

Carrie Leaney 1962-2006.

I believe it has an impact on the money we raise.

JOHN THE PUBLIC ADDRESS MAN.

My annual speech at the kick cancer event goes out live on the webcast, since Macalester now produces one for every home game. I became part of the production crew after retiring. I continued to contribute to Macalester athletics through my role as a broadcaster.

My introduction to announcing came while I was still working, when the college hosted the 1998 Division III National Track and Field Championships. All athletic staff agreed to volunteer in some way, so I offered to be the announcer. As a former head track coach, I knew the sport and that helped me immensely. I did not need to be told to allow runners to go a good fifty meters after the gun was fired before I began announcing, in case they thought my voice was a false start. I also understood how to interpret the relay races, where running the staggered curves made it difficult to determine which team was leading. I really enjoyed my time behind the microphone and was told my English accent added to the overall atmosphere of the meet.

There was a minor glitch. Some of the older coaches wanted me to convert the metric measurements of the jumping and throwing events into feet and inches. I politely informed them the track and field world had moved on.

Overall, Macalester proved to be a great host; even though many of our staff, the coaches, assistants and office workers did not know the intricacies of the sport. They still found ways to lend assistance, even if it was moving hurdles or shuttling papers to the press box. The entire meet was an unqualified success and we all knew it.

On the last day Ron Osterman, our facilities director, had a keg delivered and hidden away in the bowels of the stadium. We enjoyed a good night at the end of a demanding two-day event. Part of the satisfaction we staff members felt in contributing to the success of the meet, was that it was a one off that could so easily have been a disaster. We were not really interested in doing it again. Many of us were a little perturbed when the college petitioned to repeat the event in 2002.

I think many of us felt Macalester could not do a better job than the one we had done, so why risk our reputation. After all, we were a small Division III college, when for instance the University of St. Thomas was a much larger institution just down the street. They have a nationally competitive track team. We believed these were the types of colleges and universities who ought to host national championships. Even with the reluctance of staff members to participate, they did a great job and we succeeded in pulling it off again, minus the ecstatic feeling we had first time. It was the last time we hosted the event.

In between the two track championships hosted by Macalester, I was invited to fly to North Central University in Chicago to announce the event. I felt proud somebody appreciated my work, or perhaps I was only invited because somebody dropped out. Nonetheless there is a funny story about the Chicago meet. I was busy announcing when I noticed three female students standing nearby and staring at me. I looked at them in a way that said, 'Why are you staring?' One of the young women interpreted my questioning gaze and said "Oh, we just wanted to see who the announcer with the cool accent was." I think they left disappointed.

I announced home track meets and St. Thomas invited me to announce the MIAC championship at their stadium. I also worked at home basketball games, so I kept in touch with the athletic department through the years when I had effectively retired from competitive athletics.

I decided to retire from announcing altogether for two reasons. During my soccer webcasts I managed to do a good job while I knew the Macalester players. If I could not see the jersey numbers from the press box, I could identify them by their mannerisms. As the roster changed my job became more difficult.

There was also another problem, I needed glasses to look down and read numbers on the team sheet. I felt I was not going to do the job as well as I wanted to, so I stepped down.

RETIREMENT.

I often wonder if things had been different, if I could have chosen my retirement date. Most people know when they can retire, and they plan for it. In professions like mine however, there is often no set time.

I campaigned for our Macalester coaches to be awarded formal contracts, but most colleges hire all their staff, coaches included, by using annual appointment letters. The letters always include a paragraph which states that either party can terminate the appointment without penalty. This is one of the more despicable elements of nationwide college employment policies. I was lucky never to be subjected to the pressure of dismissal.

Coaching and the prospect of success can be addictive. Some coaches fail to see due to age or the whims of the team, it is time to retire. I honestly believe I would not have been one of them. I would have known if my team did not want to play for me and I would go.

Unfortunately, I worked with one or two coaches who believed a change in team personnel would solve their problems. Sometimes that worked, many times it did not.

I needed to retire. I had a more important commitment: my son Jack. I remain grateful that Macalester treated me graciously when I did retire.

Finally, for you Jack, some stories of golf in the hope one day you will return to this game where you have the most beautiful swing.

I am an avid golfer. During the summer I keep company at Prestwick Golf Club with other golf addicts as we try to relive our athletic glory days. In reliving mine I have an extraordinary tale to tell.

In golfing terms an eagle is two under par on any hole. They most commonly occur on par fives when a player reaches the green in two shots and holes out the putt. I have made fourteen or fifteen eagles, but I have never putted one. Four or five of them may have been chip ins on par fives, but I have had an uncommon number of eagles that I holed out from the tee or the fairway.

Showing my son Jack one of my achievements. Winning the Spring Medal at my golf club, North Manchester GC in England, 1982.

Four of these eagles were hole in ones and a story goes along with each. The first came when I was a young boy and playing the local public course, Hainault Forest. I was alone on the upper course, the easier of the two Hainault courses. It was the fifteenth hole. I hit a solid nine iron to an uphill par three, where I could not see the green. When I arrived at the green, I did not immediately see my ball, so I started looking to see if I had overshot the green, because I knew I had struck the shot well. When I failed to find it, I did what any golfer would do, I checked the hole and to my surprise I found the ball. So, what is the story?

When I was a little younger, I joined some boys who hid in the trees beside this hole, and because golfers could not see the green we ran out and put one of the balls in the hole. We then proceeded to hide and watch. I thought perhaps this trick was being played on me. But I also knew we always jumped out of hiding to make fun of the golfer, who thought he had holed out. That was the best part of the game for us. When they did not appear, and I realized what had just happened, I started jumping up and down in celebration. I had just shot my first hole in one. Unfortunately, no one else saw me do it and I did so want to show off to someone.

I made my second hole in one when I was a member at North Manchester Golf Club. I was playing with my friend Errol Davies and I holed out on number eleven. There is a longstanding tradition for a golfer who shoots a hole in one. At the end of the round he is obliged to buy everybody in the clubhouse bar a drink. However, I was playing on a Tuesday, the day the bar steward normally took off. The bar was closed. I ended up taking Errol for a pint at a local pub making it a very cheap hole in one for me.

Highland Park Golf Club in St Paul set the scene for my third. The hole does not exist now as the course has been renovated and renamed Highland National. At the time it was a course I played often because it was near where I lived and worked, Macalester College. I was playing with a friend, professor Karl Egge from the Macalester economics department. For me the eleventh hole called for an in between shot. I could use a seven or an eight iron and I understood that I had to be careful not to land in a huge bunker fronting the green. Though it was generally a safer play to use the seven iron, I chose an eight and I thought I struck it perfectly. Karl said out loud "Looks like the bunker." I immediately cursed and turned away thinking I should have used my seven iron. I failed to see the ball go into the hole. To this day, Karl regularly tells the story that I am the only player ever to have complained about making a hole in one.

There is a plaque on the wall at Highland National Golf Club for players achieving the feat of a hole in one.

My fourth hole in one came at Prestwick Golf Club in Woodbury, Minnesota, where I am currently a member. I hit a seven iron at the third hole and several players saw it go in. When we gathered at the bar, where I was obliged to buy the drinks, I told the rapidly increasing crowd I had to go pick up my son Jack at the bus stop where the school bus dropped him. I promised to return. Jack and I came back to find a larger crowd waiting expectantly for us. They all wanted a free drink.

My friend Rich Weeks greeted Jack with "Do you know your dad had a hole in one?" Jack replied, "Which hole was it?" "Number three" Rich said, "Oh, that is the easiest hole on the golf course," my son replied to gales of laughter. The drinks did not turn out to be that expensive as the club had purchased insurance. I received $500 from the insurance which greatly reduced the bill.

I have made several eagles by holing out from the fairway. Two stand out because I achieved this feat by using the same club for each shot.

Once again, I was a young boy playing the second hole on the lower course at Hainault. It is a dog leg to a short par four and there is a copse between the tee and the green. Nowadays I would probably try to drive over the trees, as it is possible to drive the green. But I was a small boy, and I decided to hit a seven iron well to the left to create a shot that would give me the same club to the green. It was a good choice. I holed out the second shot.

My favorite story of holing out from the fairway for an eagle happened at Torrey Pines South in San Diego. The seventh hole is famous now because it is where Tiger Woods defeated Rocco Mediate in a sudden death playoff to win the 2008 US Open. While Rocco and Tiger played the hole at around 500 yards it was different for me. The hole was playing around 440 yards. Though the distance was different, the hole typically played into the wind, which blew in from the ocean behind the green. The only way I could reach the green in two was if the Santa Ana winds blew from the desert turning it into a downwind hole, which it did that day. What makes this story interesting is I holed out with the same club I used as my driver, a two wood.

A golfer would immediately understand this oddity of club choice. A two wood is a relic from a bygone age. Very few Americans carry that club. But I made an eagle on a par four at Torrey Pines using a two wood for both shots. I am confident I probably did something not done in the United States for over fifty years. I use "the United States" here as I am sure the traditional golfers in the fine country of Scotland may still use the 'brassie' as the two wood is known.

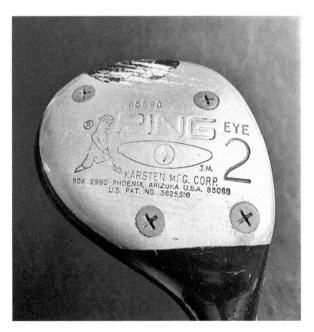

The two wood I used as my driver, originally called a 'brassie.'

I still love to play golf. Each spring I look forward to getting out on the golf course. It is all that remains of my needs and desires as an athlete and a coach.

Jack, I hope you enjoy reading this and that it helps you understand my undying love and affection for you. In memory of your Mom,

Yours,
Dad.

Lightning Source UK Ltd.
Milton Keynes UK
UKHW051932060223
416581UK00008B/570